# THE ROUGH GUIDE TO

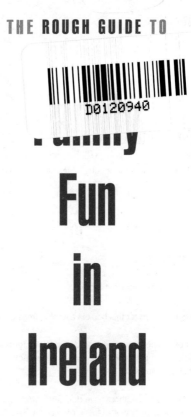

# Family Fun in Ireland

written and researched by

**Geoff Wallis and Ben West**

ROUGH
GUIDES

# Credits

Editorial and typesetting: Al Spicer
Production: John McKay
Picture research: Veneta Bullen
Cartography: Katie Lloyd-Jones

# Publishing information

Published January 2004 by Rough Guides Ltd,

80 Strand, London WC2R 0RL

© Rough Guides 2004

ISBN 1843533677

Printed in Italy by LegoPrint S.p.A

A catalogue record for this book is available from the British Library

# Contents

# Introduction

The island of Ireland may not seem the most obvious place to take your family on holiday, but in reality both North and South have plenty for families, whether it involves simply exploring the countryside, cruising on the extensive Shannon-Erne waterway, taking in the big city life of Dublin, Cork, Galway or Belfast, or just sitting back an enjoying the atmosphere of a cosy country pub. There are amazing archaeological sites like Newgrange and Dún Aengus, and dramatic, often stunning, landcapes like the Giant's Causeway and The Burren. Children are well catered for, through the number of attractions geared to their interests, and a host of possible outdoor activities from riding, angling and sailing to canoes, go-karts and mountain-bike trails. Virtually every village has its summer festival, with many providing activities and events for families, while Ireland's arts are thriving and lively and you'll never be too far away from a cinema, theatre or musical venue – indeed traditional music is one of the things kids most enjoy. There's great wildlife as well: Ireland is a birdwatcher's paradise, inhabited by a host of native and migratory birds, especially around the coast and inland waters, and you might even be lucky to spot schools of dolphins or the occasional whale basking in inshore waters. Above all, Ireland is renowned for its hospitality and friendliness: wherever you go, you and your family will be made to feel welcome. Only the weather can't be relied upon, and although the temperatures are often milder than you might expect – due to the effects of the Gulf Stream – there can be rain at any time of year. Bring rainwear, just in case.

## Accommodation

Both North and South Ireland offer possibilities to suit every budget, from luxurious hotels to the pleasures of camping or touring the country in a rented gypsy caravan. Whatever your choice, bear in mind that accommodation can be difficult to find at the time of festivals, during public holiday weekends and in the cities and major tourist areas during July and August. Fortunately, the majority of tourist offices can book you accommodation for a small fee, and there are also plenty of ways to book online. We've listed a few recommendations in the text, but bear in mind that these are just a selection – comprehensive guides are available from Tourism Ireland.

Many hotels, especially in the cities, offer a range of special deals particularly at weekends, while others, such as the *Jurys* chain, charge a price for a room, rather than per person, offering an economical choice for families. Welcoming B&Bs can be found everywhere in Ireland, most providing the traditional huge Irish breakfast, while many also have at least one room for overnight family accommodation. Below these in price are hostels, which fall into two categories – the official ones run by An Óige in the Republic and Hostelling International Northern Ireland, and the independents, many of which are members of either or both the Independent Holiday Hostels of Ireland Association or Independent Hostels Ireland. Most hostels have rooms suitable for families.

Campsites can be found all around Ireland's coastline with many inland too, especially in popular tourist areas. Most are well equipped and offer facilities such as children's play areas. Self-catering can be a very economical option, or you can rent a boat and go cruising on one of Ireland's inland waterways – several holiday companies specialize in this area.

# Sports and activities

### Birdwatching

Ireland's west and north coasts, especially islands such as Clear and Rathlin, offer the best opportunities for observing sea birds. Strangford Lough in Northern Ireland and the Wexford Slobs in the Republic's southeast are wintering grounds for various species of migratory birds. The mud flats of the east and south are home to thousands of waders and wildfowl. There's also the chance to see rare birds like the chough in the west and the corncrake in Donegal.

### Cycling

Ireland now has more than twenty waymarked cycling trails, varying in length from relatively short circuits like The Glens of Antrim Trail to more arduous, long-distance routes like The Wicklow and Wexford Tour. Details of these, cycling holiday tour companies and other information useful to cyclists can be found in the Tourism Ireland brochure, *Cycling in Ireland*. Details of bike rental outlets can be found in each chapter of this guide.

### Fishing

Hundreds of lakes and rivers provide opportunities for fly- and game-fishing. Local tourist offices can provide details of the best spots and inform you where you can get a coarse or game fishing licence and a permit from the water's owner. Virtually every port or harbour in Ireland has boats offering sea-angling trips. Tourism Ireland publishes a handy brochure.

## Gaelic football, hurling and camogie

Hurling is a fast, tough and skilful fifteen-a-side game played with a wooden hurley stick (*camán*) and a leather ball (*sliótar*) where the aim is to strike the ball into the net to score three points or hit it over the crossbar of posts similar to those in rugby to score one point. This game (and camogie, the women's version) is well worth catching. The season runs from the early summer to September and the counties where these games are most popular include Clare, Cork, Kilkenny, Offaly and Tipperary. Gaelic football shares the same pitches, scoring system and team-size as hurling, and bears similarities to both association football and rugby in that the ball can be kicked, caught and hand-passed (as in volleyball), while players can run with the ball as long as they tap it from foot to hand. Now more popular than hurling, games can be found throughout the country during the summer. For details of fixtures visit ⓦwww.gaa.ie.

## Golf and pitch and putt

Ireland's golf courses can be among the most challenging – and scenic – in the world. Tourist offices can supply the details and there are a number of companies specializing in golfing holidays. There are plenty of pitch and putt courses, too, which younger talents will enjoy, and details of these are provided in this guide. Tourism Ireland also puts out a  useful brochure.

## Horseriding and horseracing

The Irish love horses (and they love betting on them too). We've listed in each chapter the numerous opportunities for riding and trekking provided by equestrian centres. For those who love a flutter, there are plenty of race meetings and we've also provided details of the main courses.

## Walking

Ireland has waymarked long-distance trails (visit ⓦwww.irish-waymarkedways.ie for details) as well as innumerable shorter walks across a variety of different terrains, though many of the best involve hill- and mountain-walking or traversing blustery coastal paths. There are good guidebooks to help you plan longer walks, and many local tourist offices and local councils produce their own guides to walks in their area.

## Watersports

The over 3000 miles of coastline, many glorious beaches and

myriad of lakes, rivers and other waterways offer a host of opportunities for surfing, windsurfing, water-skiing or diving and getting out on the water in a yacht, canoe, kayak or rowing boat. Again Tourism Ireland publishes a booklet detailing the many companies offering water-based activities, 'Watersports in Ireland'. A clean coastline makes swimming a pleasure too, but beware of tides and dangerous undercurrents. Fortunately, the number of indoor swimming pools, especially family-oriented centres, has increased significantly, offering safe conditions whatever the weather.

# Costs and money

Gone are the days when the Republic of Ireland was a low-cost holiday destination. Over the last few years the price of tourist essentials, such as transportand eating out, has risen dramatically. However, it is still possible for the budget-conscious family to enjoy the country to the full. Away from the major tourist areas, such as Dublin, West Cork, Killarney and Galway, you'll also find your budget lasting significantly longer. Whereas the opposite used to be the case, Northern Ireland can now be a considerably cheaper place to visit than the Republic, with the exception of the cost of petrol.

## Discount cards

If you're intending to visit plenty of historic monuments, it's worth considering purchasing a discount card. In the Republic many buildings, monuments and parks are run by Dúchas, the Heritage Service (☎01/647 2453, ⓦ www.heritageireland.ie). It offers a yearly family Heritage Card for €50 which provides unlimited admission to all of its sites. In Northern Ireland, the National Trust (☎0870/458 4000) has a comparable deal with a family membership ticket costing £62.50. Although it covers far fewer attractions than Dúchas, members are also entitled to free entry to Trust properties in the rest of the UK and reduced admission prices to Dúchas sites. We've indicated in the chapters which facilities are run by Dúchas or the National Trust.

# Getting around

If you're driving your own car to Ireland, you must have a current driving licence (visitors from non-EU countries also need an International Driving Permit) and should also check that your insurance policy covers your trip; bring your vehicle registration or ownership document too. Most road signs give the place names in both Irish and English, but in Gaeltacht (Irish-speaking) areas, the names may only appear

## Currencies

The Republic of Ireland uses the Euro (€), divided into 100 cents while in Northern Ireland it is the UK pound sterling (£). At the time of writing the exchange rate was €1.37 to £1. In many border areas you will find that both currencies are accepted and even the telephone kiosks in Belfast now take Euro coins.

in Irish and be very different to the English version, so make sure you have a good map. Note that there are still some zones in Northern Ireland where it is illegal to park – if you do so, your vehicle may be regarded as a security risk.

If you're reliant solely upon public transport and planning to travel around Ireland, the Republic's Bus Éireann (ⓌWWW.buseireann.ie) and Iarnród Éireann (ⓌWWW.irishrail.ie) and the North's Ulsterbus and Northern Ireland Railways (both ⓌWWW.transco.uk) offer a variety of travel passes (children half-price). Intercity buses are mostly fast and frequent and a number of private companies offer cheaper alternatives. There is only one cross-border rail service (the Dublin–Belfast line).

Finally, cycling can be one of the most pleasant ways to explore Ireland, though it's advisable to stay well clear of the major trunk roads and avoid Dublin entirely. It's quite easy to rent a bike in the Republic, though there are far fewer rental outlets in the North. Be aware that many Irish dogs regard bicycles (and often cars too) as fair game for a chase!

# Food and drink

The range and quality of Ireland's cafés and restaurants has increased markedly over the last decade. Indeed, just about anywhere in the Republic and the North you'll be hard-pressed not to be able to find a decent meal. Many pubs also now serve food, throughout the day. Outside the larger places, the pub lunch staple is usually meat and two veg, plus plenty of potatoes, though many pubs are branching out in their menu choices. If you're staying in B&Bs, you'll usually be served the filling "traditional" Irish fried breakfast, consisting of sausages, bacon and eggs, often with a variety of different breads.

The pub is still the social focus throughout Ireland. In the Republic, opening hours are Monday to Thursday, 10.30am to 11.30pm, Friday and Saturday 10.30am to 12.30am, Sunday 12.30 to 11pm. In the North the opening times are Monday to Saturday 11.30am to 11pm, Sunday 12.30 to 10pm. Irish pubs are renowned for the "crack", that invigorating mixture of conversation and laughter, often spiced by a traditional music session. You'll find such sessions all year round in large towns and the cities and some traditional music havens, though in many

Driving around the Republic of Ireland, you'll notice that virtually every car number plate includes a letter or pair of letters indicating where it was registered. Each car number plates has three parts: the date, the county and the registration number itself, e.g. 93–DL–12345 would mean that the car was the 12,345th to be registered in County Donegal in 1993. There are 26 counties in the Republic, but Tipperary has two different pairs of letters and there are separate codes for the cities and counties of Limerick and Waterford, making 29 different index marks altogether. See how many you can spot. Dublin will be easy, but spying a number plate from a county with a small population (such as Leitrim or Roscommon) might be tricky. So keep your eyes peeled.

| | |
|---|---|
| C – Cork | LS – Laois |
| CE – Clare | MH – Meath |
| CN – Cavan | MN – Monaghan |
| CW – Carlow | MO – Mayo |
| D – Dublin | OY – Offaly |
| DL – Donegal | RN – Roscommon |
| G – Galway | SO – Sligo |
| KE – Kildare | TN – Tipperary North |
| KK – Kilkenny | TS – Tipperary South |
| KY – Kerry | W – Waterford city |
| L – Limerick city | WD – Waterford county |
| LD – Longford | WH – Westmeath |
| LH – Louth | WW – Wicklow |
| LK – Limerick county | WX – Wexford |
| LM – Leitrim | |

rural areas you'll only be likely to catch a session between June and September. Most do not begin until at least 9.30pm (and often later), though a few pubs have Sunday afternoon sessions. Unfortunately, though most pubs are generally very welcoming to children, new legislation has barred anyone under the age of 18 from being in a pub after 9pm.

# Festivals

Virtually every town and many villages have a festival of some kind at some point during the summer, many taking place over the June or August public holidays (local tourist offices will have the details). Many of these can be great fun for families, offering plenty of child–oriented events. Tourism Ireland publishes a useful Calendar of Events.

**St Patrick's Day** March 17, Ⓦwww.stpatricksfestival.ie. Celebrations all over Ireland, including parades and events, ranging from an annual horse ploughing competition in Ballycastle, Co. Antrim to a full week of activities in Dublin.

**World Irish Dancing Championships** Easter, ⓦwww.belfastcity.gov.uk. Spread over seven days held at different locations annually. The 2004 championship is in Belfast.

**North West 200** Mid-May, ☏028/7772 9869. Ireland's top motorcycle race takes place on a scenic circuit around Portrush, Co. Antrim.

**Fleadh Nua** Late May, ⓦwww.fleadhnua.com. Ennis, Co. Clare hosts this major traditional music festival.

**Medaza** 28–30 May, ☏ 021/4355152, &ⓦ www.medaza.com. Three days of world class entertainment from hot-air balloons to a whole village of bouncy castles and huge inflatable slides.

**Killarney Summerfest** Late June/early July, ⓦwww.killarneysummerfest.com. A major family festival in Co. Kerry.

**Willie Clancy Summer School of Traditional Music** Early July, ⓦwww.setdancingnews.net. Hugely popular traditional music festival, held in Miltown Malbay, Co. Clare.

**Galway Arts Festival** Mid- to late July, ⓦwww.galwayartsfestival.com. Massive festival with plenty of fun for families.

**Mary from Dungloe** Late July/early Aug, ⓦwww.maryfromdungloe.info. Ten days of fun, frolics and music in Dungloe, Co. Donegal, culminating in the selection of "Mary", and a concert by Daniel O'Donnell.

**Ballyshannon Folk and Traditional Music Festival** Early Aug, ⓦwww.ballyshannonfolkfestival.com. Lots of music and family entertainment in South Donegal.

**Puck Fair** Mid-Aug, ⓦwww.puckfair.ie. Killorglin's annual traditional fair and festival attracts participants from way beyond County Kerry's borders, especially to see a goat enthroned as king of the town.

**Kilkenny Arts Festival** Mid-Aug, ⓦwww.kilkennyarts.ie. Major ten-day festival including many events for children.

**Fleadh Cheoil na hÉireann** Late Aug, ⓦwww.comhaltas.com. Huge traditional music festival held more often than not in Listowel, Co. Kerry).

**Rose of Tralee International Festival** Late Aug, ⓦwww.roseoftralee.ie. Huge festival culminating in the crowning of the Rose in Tralee, Co. Kerry.

**Oul' Lammas Fair** Late Aug, ☏028/2076 2024. Ballycastle, Co. Antrim hosts Ireland's oldest traditional market fair with plenty of street entertainment.

**Halloween** Late Oct. Events all over Ireland but none surpasses the week of entertainment, merriment and mayhem in Derry (ⓦwww.derrycity.gov.uk/halloween).


# Fairies, legends and place names

Everybody loves a story, but probably none more so than the Irish. Indeed, the role of the *shanachie* (or story-teller) was an important part of Irish communities until recent times. Fairies

## Irish place names

Almost every Irish place name refers to some feature of the natural or built landscape and, as you tour the country, you'll keep encountering names which share certain elements. The Anglicized versions of the original often run together parts of the name and frequently change the spelling, so Arboe originated as Ard Bó, Ballycastle as Baile Chaisleáin, Killashandra as Cill na Seanrátha, and so on. Once you know some of the elements, it can be simple to work out what the place name means, for example, Bunbeg is "the little foot of the river". Many places also incorporate the name, so Inishowen comes from Inis Eoghain and means "Owen's peninsula". We've listed some of the most common below with their usual English renditions in brackets. See how many you can spot.

abhainn (avin or arvan) – river

achadh (agha) – field

ard – height

áth – ford

baile (bally) – townland, farmstead, territory

bán – white

beag (beg) – little

béal (bally or bel) – (ford-)mouth

beann (ben) – peak, summit, cliff

bó – cow

bún – bottom, foot (of a river)

carn (cairn) – cairn

carraig (carrick) – rock

ceann (kin or ken) – headland

cill (kil or kill) – church

creágan (creggan) – rocky place

cloch – stone

doire (derry) – oak-wood

droim or dromainn (drum) – ridge

dubh (dub) – black

dún – fort

eas (as, ass or es) – waterfall

fionn (fin or finn) – white, fair, bright

gall (gal) – foreigner

glas (glass) – green, grey or stream.

gleann (glen) – glen or valley

inis (innis, inish, ennis, etc) – island, peninsula or river-meadow

linn (lin) – pool

má (magh) – plain

mór (more) – big

muc (muck) – pig

muine (money) – thicket

ráth – ring-fort

rós (ross) – wood or headland

sean (shan) – old

sliabh (slieve) – mountain

sneachta (snaght) – snow

tir (tyr) – land

trá – strand, beach

play a major part in Irish legend. There are places named after them, such as the hills Sheemore and Sheebeag in County Leitrim, which literally mean "Hill of the Big Fairies" and "Hill of the Little Fairies". The banshee, which means "woman of the fairy-mound" is a rather macabre spirit who wails to warn of the imminent death of someone. The best-known fairies, of course, are the leprechauns, notorious for having a crock of gold in their possession, but, if you see one, you're unlikely to have time to lay your hands on his riches. Fairies were also thought to have the gift of song and music and there's many a tale of a musician, who walked into a fairy ring knowing just a few tunes and came out with a repertoire large enough to keep people dancing all night.

# 1

# Dublin

Set around the gorgeous sweep of Dublin Bay and divided by the River Liffey, Ireland's capital is a vibrant, thriving place with plenty to offer families. There's an abundance of attractions, including museums, castles, historic buildings and parks, and a cosmopolitan ambience about the place which draws

CENTRAL DUBLIN

King's Inns

DOMINICK

CONSTITUTION HILL

Arbour Hill Prison & Cemetery

ARBOUR HILL

KING STREET

Chimney Viewing Tower

SMITHFIELD

BOW STREET

CHURCH STREET

MARYS LANE

Collins Barracks (annexe of National Museum)

BLACKHALL PLACE

BENBURB STREET

Croppy's Acre

WOLFE TONE QUAY

Old Jameson Distillery

St Michan's

Four Courts

Heuston Station

VICTORIA QUAY

ARRAN QUAY

River Liffey

Christ Church Cathedral

MERCHANTS QUAY

St James's Gate Guinness Brewery

STEVENS LANE

BRIDGEFOOT ST

BRIDGE STREET

WINETAVERN ST

St Audoen's Churches

Dublinia

HIGH ST

CHRISTCHURCH PLACE

BOW LANE

JAMES'S STREET

THOMAS ST WEST

CORNMARKET

St Patrick's Hospital

Guinness Storehouse

CRANE ST

RAINSFORD ST

STREET

FRANCIS STREET

THE LIBERTIES

NICHOLAS ST

BACK LANE

PIMLICO

St Patrick's Cathedral

PATRICK ST

THE COOMBE

KEVIN

BLACK PITTS

NEW ST

SOUTH

LONG

N

◄ Phoenix Park

Irish Museum of Modern Art & Kilmainham Gaol ◄  Kilmainham ◄

0          400 yds

the crowds day and night. Most of Dublin is readily navigable on foot or by the excellent bus service. The countryside around is unspectacular, though along and just inland from the coast you'll find towns and villages such as Skerries, Malahide, Dún Laoghaire and Dalkey each with its own attractions, and explorable via the DART (Dublin Area Rapid Transport) system or urban rail network. Indeed, a trip on the DART from central Dublin to Killiney is well worth taking in its own right for its wonderful vistas of Dublin Bay.

## Airfield House

Upper Kilmacud Rd, Dundrum, Dublin 14; ℡ 01/298 4301; April–Sept Tues–Sun 11am–5pm; adults €4, children €2.
The nineteenth-century Airfield House and its forty-acre

estate was once owned by the Overend sisters, famous for driving around Dublin in their Rolls-Royce (now in the house's vintage car museum). All now belongs to the Airfield Trust which uses the house for exhibitions and musical events. There is now a farm where you can see animals such as goats, cows and horses, alongside ducks and hens (there's also a farmers' market every Friday here) as well as formal gardens, a picnic area and outdoor café.

## The Ark

11A Eustace St, Dublin 2; ⓣ01/670 7788, ⓦwww.ark.ie;
Opening times and charges depend upon the programme.
The Ark is a custom-built cultural centre offering an innovative programme of arts activities designed with children in

mind (and often involving children in its development). Focusing on participation and interaction, it mounts all manner of events geared towards specific age groups, including plays, exhibitions, workshops, concerts, readings and dance.

## The Bram Stoker Dracula Experience

Bar Code, Westwood Club, Clontarf Rd, Dublin 3; ⓣ01/805 7824, ⓦwww.thebramstokerdraculaexperience.com; Fri–Sun hourly noon–10pm; adults €7, children €4, family €20.

Bram Stoker, the Dublin-born author of the classic horror tale, *Dracula*, lived at 15 The Crescent, very near this new hi-tech centre devoted to both his life and his spine-tingling work. Boasting animatronic models and props, and employing one hundred gallons of imitation blood, the tour takes visitors through the Time Tunnel to Transylvania and into Dracula's Castle, where the vampire himself rests in his coffin. All should be hugely entertaining for your little horrors, but perhaps a little too realistic for the very young.

## The Chimney Viewing Tower

Smithfield Village, Dublin 7; ⓣ01/817 3800, ⓦwww.chiefoneills.com; Mon–Sat 10.30am–5.30pm, Sun 11am–5.30pm; adults €5, children €3.50, family €10.

Simply taking a trip up the side of the old Jameson Distillery chimney is exciting; a glass-panelled lift whisks you 185ft to the viewing platform. The panoramic view of the city and its countryside from here is unmatched and unforgettable.

## Dublin Zoo

Phoenix Park, Dublin 8; ⓣ01/474 8900, ⓦwww.dublinzoo.ie; March–Sept Mon–Sat 9.30am–6pm, Sun 10.30am–6pm; Oct–Feb Mon–Sat 9.30am–dusk, Sun 10.30am–dusk; adults €10.10, children €6.30 (under 3s free), family €29.40.

A trip to the zoo is always popular with the little ones and yours may have already visited their local; but what makes Dublin Zoo special is its concentration on breeding rare and endangered species for release into the wild – with the resulting new-born arrivals offering regular photo opportunities. More photo-opps are to be had on the zoo's City Farm, where children are welcome to pet and cuddle some of the more mundane of the more than seven hundred species of animals and birds represented at Phoenix Park, whose other attractions include an expansive African Plains section, plenty of big cats and primates, sea lions and penguins.

## Dublinia

St Michael's Hill, Christchurch, Dublin 8; ℡01/679 4611, ⓦwww.dublinia.ie; April–Sept daily 10am–5pm, Oct–March Mon–Sat 11am–4pm; adults €5.75, children €4.75, family €15. Dublinia's intention is to bring to life the streets of medieval Dublin and the people who bustled about them, and to a large extent it succeeds with a great deal of fun. Before you enter make sure to persuade someone to photo-

---

### Open-top Bus Tours and Bus Passes

One of the most enjoyable ways to explore Dublin is to take an open-top bus tour around the centre (for a watery alternative see p.21). Tickets for tours last for 24 hours from the time of first use, allow passengers to join the tour and hop-on and hop-off at selected stops around the city, and give discounts to admission prices at the various attractions along the route. Tickets can be purchased from the addresses below, from tourism centres, from the bus driver or online.

**Dublin Bus** 59 O'Connell St Upper, Dublin 1; ℡01/873 4222, ⓦwww.dublinbus.ie. Tours run every day of the year at ten minute intervals 9.30am–5pm and every thirty minutes 5–6.30pm, commencing from outside. Commentary is provided by often very witty (and sometimes even singing) drivers. Adults €12.50, children €6. As an alternative for the independently minded, Dublin Bus offers a number of different travel passes. The **Family One-Day Rambler** costs €7.50. There's also a variety of **Adult Rambler** passes ranging from one day (€5) to seven days (€17.50). Children under 16 can get a seven-day **Travelwide pass** (€5), though those over 12 require a Schoolchild Photo ID from the Dublin Bus office.

**Irish City Tours** 33 Bachelors Walk, Dublin 1; ℡01/782 9010, ⓦwww.irishcitytours.com. Daily tours every fifteen minutes from 9.30am with the last tour leaving at 5.30pm from mid-July to Sept, 5pm from April to mid-July and during October, and 4pm Nov–March. Tours commence from outside 12 O'Connell Street Upper and commentary is given by an expert guide.

graph you in the stocks outside the building. Inside you'll discover various shops and stalls where you can ogle the pies, try on clothes and have a go at brass rubbing, not forgetting to test your throwing skills at another set of stocks. You can marvel too at a rather gruesome Black Death tableau before examining some of the findings from the excavations of Wood Quay, including human and animal remains. Finally, there's a steep climb to the top of St Michael's Tower for a view of the surrounding area (albeit through rather grubby windowpanes).

## The GAA Museum

Croke Park, Dublin 3; ⓣ 01/855 8176, ⓦ www.gaa.ie; Mon–Sat 9.30am–5pm, Sun noon–5pm (closed on match days); adults €5, children €3, family €13 (including stadium tour adults €8.50, children €5, family €21).

Croke Park is the headquarters of the Gaelic Athletic Association and a stadium whose capacity of more than 80,000 spectators makes it the fourth largest in Europe. Housed under the main stand, its excellent museum takes you through the history of the sports of hurling and Gaelic football, offering enthralling displays and plenty of touch-screen interaction. Best of all, however, are the chances to try your skills at whacking a *camán* (hurling ball) with a *sliotar* (hurling stick) and testing your reactions at catching a ball.

## Guinness Storehouse

St James's Gate, Dublin 8; ⓣ 01/408 4800, ⓦ www.guinness-storehouse.com; daily 9.30am–5pm; adults €13.50, children aged 6–12 €3, under 6s free, family €28.

Even if your children haven't driven you to drink, you should bring them here; it's a seven-storey temple to all things connected with the black stuff (more than two and a half million pints of which are produced daily) that takes visitors on a self-guided trip through the drink's manufacturing process, replete with cascades of water, vast barrels and a surviving engine from the plant's old railway. It's a thoroughly noisy, gargantuan place which gives children a real and fun insight into the reason their parents are always thirsty in Ireland. The second floor houses a collection of memorabilia, including advertisements both old and more recent (including a fascinating selection of comic videos) and also the eighteenth-century Downhill Harp, a version of the classic brass-strung instrument on which the Guinness logo is based. Tours end at the seventh floor Gravity Bar which offers not only a pint of what some reckon to be the best Guinness in Dublin (included in the admission price, but only for those over 18) but a stunning panorama of the city and surrounding countryside.

# Irish Museum of Modern Art

Royal Hospital, Military Rd, Kilmainham, Dublin 8; ℗01/612 9900, ⓦwww.modernart.ie; Tues–Sat 10am–5.30pm, Sun noon–5.30pm; free.

Housed in the seventeenth-century Royal Hospital, set in splendid grounds, the museum hosts a varied programme of exhibitions, some of which may be of interest to older children. On Sundays (2–5pm; free) IMMA offers drop-in art exploration sessions for families, involving a range of different art-making projects.

# Kilmainham Gaol

Inchicore Rd, Kilmainham, Dublin 8; ℗01/453 5984, ⓦwww.heritageireland.ie; April–Sept daily 9.30am–5pm; Oct–March Mon–Sat 9.30am–4pm, Sun 10am–5pm; adults €5, children €2, family €11; Heritage card.

One of the most startling visitor attractions in the whole of Ireland, Kilmainham Gaol functioned as a rigorous house of punishment and correction from 1796 to 1924. Its notoriety lies in the fact that leaders of every Irish rebellion between 1798 and 1916 were incarcerated here, while the last prisoner to be released was Éamon de Valera in 1924, subsequently to become Ireland's Taoiseach (prime minister) and later its president. Guided tours take place every 45 minutes, so, if you're early, do make sure to take in the gaol's fascinating exhibition which provides much background information on how the prison was run, prisoners' conditions, nineteenth-century crime (including an early "mugshot" camera) and the various struggles for independence. The tour itself takes in the tiers of cells which form the East Wing, the prison Chapel and the harsh and cramped conditions of the West Wing, together with a short, but evocative video on the prison's history and the yacht Asgard, used by Erskine Childers and his sister Molly to smuggle guns into Ireland in 1914. Bear in mind that there was no heating in the prison and there still isn't, so wrap up well, if you're visiting in winter.

# Lambert Puppet Theatre

5 Clifton Lane, Monkstown, Co. Dublin; ℗01/280 0964.

This theatre stages daily shows during May and June (call for times) and all year performances on Saturdays and Sundays at 3.30pm. The Saturday show is especially suitable for children aged 4 and above (€6.35).

# Malahide Castle, the Fry Model Railway and Tara's Palace

Malahide, Co. Dublin; ℗01/846 2184, ⓦwww.visitdublin.com, April–Oct Mon–Sat 10am–12.45pm & 2pm–5pm, Sun 11am–12.45pm & 2–6pm; Nov–March Mon–Sat 10am–12.45pm

& 2–5pm, Sun 11am–12.45pm & 2–5pm; adults €6, children
€3.50, family €16.50.

Malahide began life in the late twelfth century as a tower
house belonging to the Talbots. They retained possession for
the next eight hundred years, modifying and expanding it
from an easily defended stronghold into a comfortable, ram-
bling home. Even so, in 1973, when the last of the line passed
away, Malahide was still a castle, and it keeps the romantic
look and feel of a fortress. Today it defends nothing more
than an interesting collection of art and a jumble of architectural styles, pointed out during the guided tours. Look out
for the small entranceway in the corner of the Great Hall
known as "Puck's Door" named for a servant who reputedly
slept through an attack by invaders and hung himself in
shame, and whose ghost is believed to appear whenever
changes threaten the castle.

The castle is also home to the Fry Model Railway (℡01/846
3779, ⓦwww.visitdublin.com; April–Sept Mon–Sat
10am–1pm & 2–5pm; adults €6, children €3.50, family
€16.50), the biggest in Ireland, covering almost 300 square
yards. Its handmade models, some of which date back to the
1920s and 1930s, show the diversity of Ireland's transportation
system. So you won't find just plenty of trains from different
periods of railway history (including the DART) and assorted
railway paraphernalia here, but also a system centred upon the
River Liffey replete with bridges and barges.

Your visit to Malahide should also include Tara's Palace
(℡01/846 3779; April–Sept Mon–Sat 10am–1pm & 2–5pm,
Sun 2–6pm; recommended minimum donation – adults €2,
children €1). Next to the Fry Model Railway, the Palace is
an astonishing, meticulously created dolls' house, built to one
twelfth scale and inspired by genuine eighteenth-century
mansions. Intricately furnished – there are real paintings
hanging on its elegant walls and exquisite ornamentations
grace its furniture and decor – it includes a chapel and a bil-
liards room. Also on display is a range of other antique dolls'
houses, including one owned by Oscar Wilde's mother, and a
selection of toys dating back to as far as 1720.

## National Gallery of Ireland

Merrion Square West, Dublin 2; ℡ 01/661 5133, ⓦ www.national-
gallery.ie; Mon–Sat 9.30am–5.30pm (Thurs until 8.30pm), Sun
noon–5.30pm; free.

The gallery's education department (℡01/663 3505) mounts
an extensive range of activities for children, including the
Family Programme (Feb–June & Sept–Nov Sat 3pm; free)
which offers opportunities for adults and children (aged
5–12) to explore art together through activities such as story-
telling, craftwork and music. Additionally, there is a regular
Children's Sunday Talk each week at 12.30pm, suitable for a

similar age range, on a variety of art-related subjects and special workshops in July for children aged 3–6 (Mon–Fri 11am–noon; €5 per class, €20 per week).

## National Museum of Ireland – Archaelogy and History

Kildare St, Dublin 2; ⓣ01/677 7444, ⓦwww.museum.ie; Tues–Sat 10am–5pm, Sun 2–5pm; free.

Housing a wealth of prehistoric, Viking and medieval finds, as well as an Egyptian gallery, the National Museum's archaeological and historical collection offers an astonishing array of objects and artefacts many of which will be of interest to children. It's Ór gallery is dedicated to prehistoric golden treasures, while the Prehistoric Ireland section incorporates a reconstruction of a Neolithic passage tomb, including decorated stones from Newgrange. In the Viking Ireland gallery you'll discover the skeleton of a warrior alongside various rings and brooches, models of a Viking Dublin house and plenty of objects excavated from the city's Winetavern Street and Wood Quay. Medieval Ireland focuses on subjects as varied as weaponry and worship, as well as exhibits of games and a keg of bog butter. The small Egyptian room naturally includes mummies (always a winner), as well as hieroglyphic scripts and an astonishingly detailed model of a Nile boat. The Museum's Education and Outreach Department (ⓣ01/648 6453) runs a regular programme of events for children aged 7 upwards and activity sheets are available at the museum's reception.

## National Museum of Ireland – Decorative Arts and History

Collins Barracks, Benburb St, Dublin 7; ⓣ01/677 7444, ⓦwww.museum.ie; Tues–Sat 10am–5pm, Sun 2–5pm; free.

Housed in barracks dating from 1701, which surround the biggest drill square in Europe (capable of holding six regiments), the National Museum's Decorative Arts has some exhibits which may be of interest to older children (and activity sheets, suitable for 9–13 year olds are available at reception). The most intriguing selection is contained within the Curator's Choice gallery which includes eighteenth-century musical instruments as well as the cabinet given by Oliver Cromwell to his daughter as a wedding present. The Out of Storage gallery includes an striking seventeenth-century Japanese suit of armour and elsewhere you'll find intriguing clocks, scientific instruments, an impressive Victorian dolls' house and The Way We Wore exhibition, tracing 250 years of Irish clothing. The museum runs a programme of events and activities for children of various ages once or twice a month (Sun 3–4pm) based around the exhibits.

# National Museum of Ireland – Natural History Collection

Merrion St, Dublin 2; Ⓣ 01/677 7444, ⓦ www.museum.ie;
Tues–Sat 10am–5pm, Sun 2–5pm; free.

Known to Dubliners as the "Dead Zoo" thanks to its vast collection of stuffed animals and birds and skeletons, a visit to the Natural History Museum is always a great day out for the children. The collection focuses on Irish wildlife on its ground floor including skeletons of the giant Irish deer, which became extinct around 9000BC. The first floor houses the World Collection which includes all manner of simians, a rhinoceros and giraffes. Further upstairs, there's a stuffed dodo and a good vantage point to view the skeletons of two whales, once beached on Irish shores, which hang from the ceiling. There are various activity sheets to guide young minds through the galleries, and make something special of what might otherwise be "just another museum". The sheets are free at the ground floor reception desk, where you'll also be able to pick up details of the Saturday Club (11am–noon) and Sunday activities sessions (3–4pm), together with the regularly changing programme of events they offer.

## National Transport Museum

Heritage Depot, Howth Castle Demesne, Howth, Co. Dublin;
Ⓣ 01/832 0427, ⓦ www.nationaltransportmuseum.org.
June–Aug Mon–Sat 10am–5pm, Sept–May Sat & Sun 2–5pm;
adults €3, children €1.50, family €8.

Housed in a converted barn in the grounds of Howth Castle (not open to the public), the museum is home to buses and trams, fire engines and horse-drawn conveyances that add a vivid reality to children's view of the past. It's run by enthusiasts who proudly display photographs and transport memorabilia alongside the weird and wonderful vehicles.

## National Wax Museum

Granby Row, Parnell Square, Dublin 1; Ⓣ 01/872 6340; Mon–Sat 10am–5.30pm, Sun noon–5.30pm; adults €6, children €4, family €18.

Boasting more than three hundred exhibits, from Madonna to the Teletubbies, the Wax Museum is an enjoyable place to pass a couple of hours on a wet afternoon. Younger children will delight in the World of Fairytale and Fantasy and their quest for the magical lamp, while there are also plenty of tunnels to crawl through and a hall of mirrors. Older children will probably be absorbed by the Chamber of Horrors and, of course, there's always the opportunity to be photographed next to your favourite hero or heroine. For adults there's a recreation of Da Vinci's *Last Supper*, literary figures, such as Joyce and Yeats, and a line-up of Irish prime ministers, featuring an incredibly sinister-looking Charles Haughey.

## Newbridge House and Traditional Farm

Donabate, Co. Dublin; ⊤01/843 6534; April–Sept Tues–Sat
10am–1pm & 2–5pm, Sun 2–6pm; Oct–March Sat & Sun 2–5pm;
adults €6, children aged 12–18 €5, children aged 3–11 €3.50,
family €16.50.

While adults will relish a tour of this splendid Georgian mansion, dating from 1737, and admire its Rococo plasterwork
and antique decor and furniture, the key attractions for children are the Museum of Curiosities and the Traditional
Farm. The former includes such oddities as an arcane
Kashmiri sari box and a clutch of ostrich eggs laid in
Dundalk. The house's courtyard also includes a dairy, carpen-
ter's shop and blacksmith's forge, all equipped with appropri-
ate implements, while the farm is stocked with a variety of
traditional animals.

## North Bull Island

Accessed via Bull Bridge, off Clontarf Rd, Dublin 3, or the causeway leading from Watermill Rd, Dublin 5.

Apart from featuring the delights of the three-mile
Dollymount Strand on its seaboard side, North Bull Island
provides a temporary winter home to an enormous number
of migratory birds, including one-sixth of the world's population of Brent Geese. In summer, sea birds such as cormorants
and oystercatchers are plainly visible while the island is also
rich in wildflowers and inhabited by that increasing rarity the
Irish hare. You can learn more about the island and its residents at the Interpretive Centre by the beach at the end of
the causeway (daily 10am–4.30pm; free).

## Phoenix Park Visitor Centre

Phoenix Park, Dublin 8; ⊤01/677 0095,
Ⓦwww.heritageireland.ie; Jan to mid-March and Nov & Dec Sat
& Sun 10am–5pm, mid- to end-March and Oct daily
10am–5.30pm, April–Sept daily 10am–6pm; adults €2.75, children €1.25, family €7.

Spread over 1760 acres, Phoenix Park is the largest urban
park in Europe and would take several days to explore fully.
Home to Dublin Zoo (see above), the park also has its own
herd of three hundred deer which can sometimes be seen
roaming to the southwest of the Phoenix Memorial. The
park is dotted with cricket, football and hurling pitches and
polo fields, as well as including the Áras an Uachtaráin (the
official residence of the Irish president) and the 92ft-high
stainless steel Papal Cross, situated on the spot where Pope
John Paul II celebrated Mass with a congregation of a million
and a quarter people in September, 1979. The park's visitor
centre, near the northern Ashtown Gate, is a great place to
begin your visit; it has a child-oriented exhibition looking at

the park's wildlife and illustrating the four and a half thousand years of history represented by the Knockmaree cist – an ancient grave found in the park in 1838 and reconstructed here.

Admission to the Visitor Centre also includes a tour of the adjacent Ashtown Castle, a seventeenth-century tower house, whose defensive features include a "murder hole" and a staircase with a "trip step".

## St Michan's Church

Church St, Dublin 7; ⊤ 01/872 4154; March–Oct Mon–Fri 10am–12.30pm & 2–4.30pm, Sat 10am–12.45pm; Nov–March Mon–Fri 12.30–3.30pm, Sat 10am–12.45pm; adults €3.50, children €2.50.

Dating from 1095, St Michan's is the Northside's oldest surviving building, though much of it was rebuilt in 1685. The vaults of its crypt have achieved renown thanks to the presence of a dozen bodies preserved by the dry environment (the limestone walls absorb moisture), constant temperature and methane generated by rotting vegetation beneath the church. Thought to be between 300 and 700 years old, the corpses include a woman reputed to have been be a nun, a man missing a hand and an alleged Crusader – perfect material for your bloodthirsty brood to dwell on. Other vaults include the coffins of the Shears brothers, executed for their part in the 1798 Rebellion, and the death-mask of the Rebellion's leader, Wolfe Tone. The tours are superbly informative and vary in duration according to the whim and humour of the guide, but visitor numbers are strictly limited.

## St Stephen's Green

Dublin 2, Mon–Sat 8am–dusk, Sun 10am–dusk; free.

The centre of the most renowned and largest of Dublin's Georgian squares is occupied by a pleasant park whose gardens were originally laid out in 1880 for Lord Ardilaun (previously known as Sir Arthur Guinness) who donated the park to the people of Dublin. Featuring flower gardens, herbaceous borders, a bandstand occasionally used for outdoor concerts and a lake full of waterfowl, the park makes an ideal spot for a summer picnic or simply just a stroll.

## Skerries Watermill and Windmills

Miller's Lane, Skerries, Co. Dublin; ⊤ 01/849 5208, ⓦ http://indigo.ie/~skerries; daily 10.30am–5.30pm (Oct–March closes 4.30pm); adults €5, children €4, family €10.

Set in the centre of Skerries Town Park, this complex features two windmills, a watermill complete with millraces and ponds alongside a field to provide grain for grinding. Visitors can see the machinery in action, learn about its history and have a go at grinding some corn. The tea rooms here offer a broad range of musical entertainment, from traditional music to jazz, each Sunday lunchtime (Sept–May noon–2pm).

## Trinity College Library and The Dublin Experience

College St, Dublin 2; ⓣ 01/608 2320, ⓦ www.tcd.ie/library/; library: all year Mon–Sat 9.30am–5pm, also June–Sept Sun 9.30am–4.30pm and Oct–May Sun noon–4.30pm; adults €7, children €6, family €14; The Dublin Experience: late May to early Oct daily 10am–5pm; adults €4.20, children €3.50.

Ireland's oldest university, founded in 1592, is also the country's most popular tourist attraction. The reason is the Book of Kells, a fabulous ninth-century illustrated manuscript which forms the focus of the context-placing exhibition *Turning Darkness into Light* in the Old Library, though the book itself is displayed in the Treasury. The College's Arts and Social Sciences building houses the 45-minute audiovisual show, The Dublin Experience, which takes its audience through a thousand years of Dublin's history.

## Viking Splash Tour on land and water

64–65 Patrick St, Dublin 8; ⓣ 01/707 6000, ⓦ www.vikingsplash-tours.com; Feb–Nov ten tours daily except Feb–May & Nov Tues; Feb–June & Sept–Nov Mon–Fri adults €13.95, children €7.95, family €47; Feb–Nov Sat & Sun and July & Aug Mon–Fri adults €15.95, children €8.95, family €58.

For a truly different city tour a trip on one of Viking Splash's reconditioned World War Two amphibious vehicles known as "Ducks" is essential. The one-and-a-quarter-hour tour sets off from Bull Alley and trundles around the city's sites and attractions before plunging into the waters of the Grand Canal Dock and taking a leisurely return trip along the River Liffey (don't panic, you won't get wet). Tours last an hour and a quarter and tickets may also be purchased at tourist centres.

## Waterways Visitor Centre

Grand Canal Quay, Dublin 2; ⓣ 01/677 7510, ⓦ www.waterways.org; June–Sept daily 9.30am–5.30pm, Oct–May Wed–Sun 12.30–5pm; adult €2.50, child €1.20, family €6.35.

The best way to approach the Visitor Centre is by taking a stroll along the banks of the Grand Canal which forms a loop around the inner Southside (see below). The Centre itself provides an entertaining account of Ireland's inland waterways, including samples of art and literature inspired by them, and various working models, such as a barge passing through a lock. If you've considering a holiday afloat, there's a video which recounts some of the most scenic attractions of the

## A walk around the Grand Canal

There are dozens of agreeable stolls to be had on the highways and byways of Dublin, but a walk along the banks of the Grand Canal is particularly pleasant because of the mixture of land and water it offers. The official Grand Canal Way comprises a three-and-a-half-mile loop commencing at the Waterways Visitor Centre before passing through leafy suburbs replete with pleasant Victorian architecture. South of Baggot Street Bridge look out for the statue of the poet Patrick Kavanagh while, by Portobello Bridge, Portobello College originated as the Grand Canal Hotel in 1807, serving as a terminus for passenger barges which plied the canal. The walk ends at the junction of Dolphin Road and Spur Road, the latter leading to Kilmainham Gaol.

waterways and the Centre also sells all manner of related guides, navigation charts and towpath trails.

# Sport and activities

### Bike rental

We can't recommend that anyone cycles in Dublin; the traffic is far too dangerous. If you plan to head out of town, however, or spend a Sunday exploring Phoenix Park, then Cycle Ways, Parnell St, Dublin 1, ℡01/837 4748, are the people you want.

### Cinemas

**Savoy**, O'Connell Street Upper, Dublin 1, ℡01/874 6000, ⓦwww.filminfo.net; **Screen Cinema**, D'Olier Street, Dublin 2, ℡01/672 5500, ⓦwww,filminfo.net; **UGC**, Parnell St, Dublin 1, ℡01/872 8444.

### Gaelic football and Hurling

Major games, including the All-Ireland Finals in September, take place at Croke Park, ℡01/836 3222.

### Go-karting

**Kylemore Indoor Karting**, Unit 1A, Kylemore Industrial Estate, Killeen Rd, Dublin 10; ℡01/626 1444, ⓦwww.kylemore-karting.com; Daily 11am–10pm. Ireland's largest indoor karting arena offers a choice of two almost 400-yard long tracks, each featuring hills, banked corners, flyovers and underpasses. Full instruction is given and helmets, gloves and race suits are provided. Ten minutes' practice on a single track costs €15, rising to €30 for 25 minutes or you can try 15 minutes on both tracks for €30. There's a special race for 9–14 year olds (€20) each Sunday at 10am. A deposit of €100 is required when booking.

## Horseracing

**Leopardstown Racecourse,** Foxrock, Co. Dublin; ℡ 01/289 3607, Ⓦ www.leopardstown.com; Weekends throughout the year and Wednesday evenings in summer. There are also other racecourses close to Dublin, such as Punchestown, in Naas.

## Leisureplex centres

Blanchardstown, Dublin 15; ℡ 01/822 3030; Malahide Rd, Coolock, Dublin 17, ℡ 01/848 5722; Old Bray Rd, Stillorgan, Co. Dublin, ℡ 01/288 1656; Village Green Centre, Tallaght, Dublin 24, ℡ 01/459 9411; Ⓦ www.leisureplex.ie; Daily 12am–12pm. Each centre features The Zoo (an adventure play area, including a separate space for toddlers, ten pin bowling and a live action laser game. The Blanchardstown centre also has dodgems.

## Swimming

**Markievicz Leisure Centre**, Townsend St, Dublin 2; ℡ 01/672 9121; Ⓦ www.dublincity.ie; Mon–Thurs 7am–9pm, Fri 7am–7pm, Sat 9am–5pm, Sun 10am–3pm; adults €4.70, children €2.60 (under 2s free), family €8.50. Sessions last 45 minutes and commence on the hour. Open swimming sessions usually take place Mon–Fri, 9–11am & 2–4pm and Sat & Sun all day. Under 18s must be supervised by an adult.
**National Aquatic Centre**, Snugborough Rd, Blanchardstown, Dublin 15; ℡ 01/646 4300, Ⓦ www.nac.ie; Leisure pool July & Aug Mon–Fri 9am–9pm, Sat & Sun 9am–8pm; Sept–June Mon–Fri 1–9pm, Sat & Sun 9am–8pm; adults e*11, children e*9. As well as offering a competition pool for serious swimmers (call for times), the NAC's leisure pool includes a water roller coaster, surfing machine, wave and bubble pools, a pirate's ship and the Dark Hole Flume water slide. There's a special session for families (Sat 9–10am) and under 8s must be accompanied in the water by an adult at all times.

## Theatres

**The Abbey Theatre**, Abbey St Lower, Dublin 1, ℡ 01/878 7222, Ⓦ www.abbeytheatre.ie; **Gaiety Theatre**, King St South, Dublin 2, ℡ 01/677 1717, wwww.gaietytheatre.com; **Gate Theatre**, 1 Cavendish Row, Parnell Square, Dublin 1, ℡ 01/874 4045, Ⓦ www.gate-theatre.ie; **Olympia Theatre**, 72 Dame St, Dublin 2, ℡ 01/677 7744, Ⓦ www.olympia.ie;

# Accommodation

**Central Hotel**, 2–5 Exchequer St, Dublin 2; ℡01/679 7302, ⓦwww.centralhotel.ie; As its name suggests, this is in a prime central location; there's a single family room from €130.

**Clifden Guesthouse**, 32 Gardiner Place, Dublin 1; ℡01/874 6364, ⓦwww.clifdenhouse.com; Comfortable, family-run establishment offering family accommodation from around €120 per night.

**Jurys Inn Christchurch**, Christchurch Place, Dublin 8; ℡01/607 0000, ⓦwww.bookajurysinn.com; Popular with families, thanks to its inclusive room rates. Rooms can accommodate two adults and two children and prices commence at €103.

**Jacob's Inn**, 21–28 Talbot Place, Dublin 1; ℡01/855 5660, ⓦwww.isaacs.ie; One of the best-equipped Dublin hostels, offering en suite rooms from €24 per person.

**Leeson Inn**, 24 Leeson St Lower, Dublin 2; ℡01/662 2002, ⓦwww.iol.ie/leesoninn. Elegant four-storey Georgian townhouse with very competitive rates from around €50 per person (children under twelve sharing with adults stay free).

**Oliver St John Gogarty Apartments**, 18–21 Anglesea St, Temple Bar, Dublin 2; ℡01/671 1822. Well worth considering for larger families wanting several days in Dublin, these self-catering apartments sleep four people and cost from €160 per night.

# Places to eat

**Beshoff's**, 14 Westmoreland St, Dublin 2, and 6 O'Connell St Upper, Dublin 1. Excellent sit-down fish and chips.

**Bewley's Oriental Café**, Grafton St & Westmoreland St, Dublin 2. A Dublin insitution serving everything from excellent coffee, sticky buns, sandwiches and cakes to full breakfasts, lunches and dinners.

**Botticelli**, 3 Temple Bar, Dublin 2. Excellent pizza plus its own ice-cream parlour.

**Café Kylemore, S**t Stephen's Green Shopping Centre, Dublin 2 and Earl Street, Dublin 1. Child-friendly self-service restaurants which offer a daily changing menu.

**Captain America's**, 44 Grafton St, Dublin 2, for a variety of steaks, chicken, burgers, seafood and vegetarian meals consumed within walls festooned with rock music memorabilia.

**Elephant and Castle**, 18 Temple Bar, Dublin 2. Hugely popular upmarket burger restaurant also offering Cajun and Creole cuisine.

**O'Shea's**, 23 Anglesea St, Temple Bar, Dublin 2. Popular family restaurant specializing in traditional Irish meals.

# 2

# Wicklow and Kildare

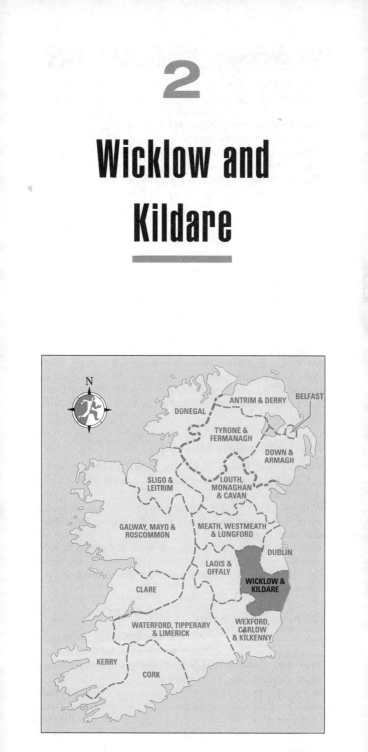

Kildare lies just west of Dublin, and Wicklow just to the south of the city, making this part of Ireland very accessible indeed. The Dublin light rail network, the DART, goes out as far as Greystones on the Wicklow coast, and the main line continues to Arklow; and most of the major tourist centres are served by buses. In Kildare, the railway more or less follows the major N4 and N7 roads and serves many of the sights.

Wicklow and Kildare offer a rural respite from the hectic capital. They have great opportunities for walking and cycling, as well as marvellous golden, sandy beaches for relaxing seaside days. More energetic families will love the wild, desolate Wicklow Mountains traversing the 82-mile way-marked Wicklow Way, whilst Kildare explores one of Ireland's major industries, racehorse-breeding, at the National Stud in Kildare town.

## Arklow Maritime Museum

St Mary's Road, Arklow, Co. Wicklow; ⓣ 0402/32868; summer Mon–Sat 10am–1pm & 2–5pm; adults €7, students €3, children under 12 free.

A three-minute walk from the tourist office, the museum traces the town's history from when the Vikings established the town in the ninth century. The video presentation is worth watching but the main attraction is the splendidly varied collection which includes tools, models (with a ship made from more than 10,000 matchsticks), a whale's tooth and its eardrum.

## Glenroe Open Farm

Ballygannon, Kilcoole, Co. Wicklow; ⓣ 01/287 2288, ⓦ www.glenroefarm.com; March, Sept and Oct, Sat–Sun 10am–5pm; April–Aug Mon–Fri 10am–5pm, Sat–Sun 10am–6pm; adults €4.25, children €3.50, family €14.

A charming stop just off the N11 main road about 20 miles south of Dublin, Glenroe offers a display of historic farm implements, and the chance to get close to farm animals such as donkeys, horses, goats, sheep, and pigs. Those with softer hearts will enjoy cooing at the peacocks, rabbits, deer and other smaller fry on show. The coffee shop, picnic areas and outdoor playground will calm the over-excited before the return to base.

## National Sea Life Centre

Strand Road, Bray, Co. Wicklow; ☎ 01/286 6939, ⓦ www.sealife.ie; Mon–Fri 10am–4pm, Sat & Sun 10am–5pm/Easter–Sept daily 10am–5pm, weekends only rest of year; reduced hours in winter; adults €8, children €5.50, family €22.

The main attraction on the Bray seafront, this hi-tech, child-orientated aquarium successfully disguises serious educational material as entertainment for the whole family. It specializes in Irish marine life and can boast exhibits including sharks, octopus, a rock tunnel carved by a freshwater stream, and a touch pool with crabs and starfish. There's a subtle focus on conservation throughout the visit as children are quizzed using "magic" glasses to read coded questions and find answers on special scratchpads.

## Powerscourt Estate and Waterfall

Enniskerry, Co. Wicklow; ☎ 01/204 6000; ⓦ www.powerscourt.ie; house & gardens daily: March–Oct 9.30am–5.30pm; Nov–Feb 9.30am–dusk; waterfall daily: summer 9.30am–7pm; winter 9.30am–dusk; house and garden: adults €8 summer/€6.50 winter, children €4.50 summer/€3.50 winter, under 5s free; waterfall adults €3.50, children over 5 €1.80.

This partly restored eighteenth-century Palladian mansion some twelve miles south of Dublin off the N11, this is one of Ireland's grandest estates, with a Japanese garden, walled garden and other magnificent formal gardens with a backdrop of the Wicklow hills.

The kids will enjoy climbing the Pepper Pot Tower and the great views it offers, and some of them will relish the pet cemetery. The house itself is less of a must-see as it now functions mainly as a shopping centre, but the terraced café and picnic area make good resting points. The playground nearby is worth looking in on if there's excess energy to burn off before the four-mile signposted walk through the estate.

A three-mile drive following signs along the road takes you to the highest waterfall in Ireland (daily: summer 9.30am–7pm; winter 10.30am–dusk; €3.50), where the quiet River Dargle turns suddenly angry before plunging some 400ft into the valley below. Mother Nature's other local attractions are highlighted along the nature trail that runs around the base of the fall; at less than a mile, it makes a suitably low-stress end to an exciting visit.

## Clara Lara Fun Park

11 Glenmalure Pines, Greenan, Rathdrum, Co. Wicklow;
Ⓣ0404/46161; May–Aug 10am-6pm; adults €7, children €3
under 4s free, additional charges for some activities.

This outdoor adventure park by the Avonmore River prom-
ises a feast of water-based fun and mini golf. Try your hand at
go-karting, hill walking, rafting or canoeing while the rest of
the family explores the treehouses, wooden playgrounds,
pirate galleon and water slides. Summer visits are great for
barbecues and picnics, and Santa Claus visits in December;
phone for details.

## Avondale House and Forest Park

Rathdrum, Co. Wicklow; Ⓣ0404/46111,
Ⓦwww.coillte.ie/tourism_and_recreation-
2003/avondale_home_parnell.htm; mid-March–Oct, daily
11am–6pm (House closed Mon March–April, Sept–Oct); House
€5, family €15.

This splendid Georgian house, built in 1777, has been
restored to the decor of circa 1850. Now a museum to political leader Charles Stewart Parnell (1846-91), it is set in magnificent forested grounds. Children will enjoy romping up
and down the nature trails, where badgers, otters and ninety
species of birds and other wildlife may be spotted, and will
adore the residents of the deer pen. For rest, recuperation and
the like, there is a picnic area, play area, a gift shop and café.

## Wicklow Historic Gaol

Kilmartin Hill, Wicklow Town; Ⓣ0404/61599, Ⓦwww.wicklowshis-
toricgaol.com; mid-April–Sept, daily 10am–6pm, tours every 10
min; adults €5.80, children €3, family with up to 3 children €15.

Times were hard for criminals in the eighteenth century. This
gaol was built in 1702 with more than 400 inmates sharing
the 42 cells: they were fed once every four days and allowed
15 minutes' exercise in the prison yard per month. The costumed guides offer a lively re-creation of the grim prison
conditions, and make a powerful impression on children, who
soon learn that in the eighteenth and nineteenth centuries
they would have been welcomed to stay just as readily as
adults. Tours last 60–90 minutes and focus on the role the
gaol played after the 1798 rebellion and on the lives of those
sent from here to the colonies.

## Larchill Arcadian Garden

Kilcock, Co. Kildare; Ⓣ01/628 7354, Sept Sat & Sun noon–6pm,
June–Aug Tues–Sun noon–6pm; adults €7, children €5, family
€25, free for under 4s.

On the Dunshaughlin Road signposted off the N4 main road

near Maynooth, this 63-acre parkland contains Europe's only surviving ornamental farm – the precursor to the modern landscaped garden – and is a feast of decorative buildings, statuary, water features and a lake with castle follies. Of more immediate interest to younger members of the family, it also has nature trails, a splendid wooden adventure trail, and indoor play area. There's a puppet theatre, magic shows on Saturdays, a maze in summer, a walled garden with peacocks, and animals galore on the farm – including llamas! A ghost haunts the cockle-shell-covered tower, and there is also a pet corner, sandpit, playground with old fashioned games and a café.

## Irish National Stud

Kildare Town; ☎ 045/521617, ⓦ www.irish-national-stud.ie; mid–Feb to mid–Nov daily 9.30am-6pm, last admission 5pm; guided tours on the hour from 11am; adults €8.50, children over 12 €6.50, children under 12 €4.50, family €18.

Those not yet old enough to invest speculatively on the relative speed of the animals living here will still find a visit to the National Stud fascinating. This is the heart of the Irish racing world, and a trip to the Stud, on the Tully Estate on the south side of Kildare, signposted from the town centre, is the best way to get close to the breeding, training and attention to detail that makes Irish horses so supremely valuable. As well as the thoroughbreds themselves, you'll get to see stallion boxes, a museum and a spotlessly clean complex of white buildings set amongst green lawns and overshadowed by the bleak ruins of the Black Abbey. Don't miss the ornate Japanese Garden and tranquil St Fiachra's Garden, a beautiful place of lakes and monastic cells.

## Lullymore Heritage and Discovery Park

Lullymore, Co. Kildare; ☎ 045/870238; ⓦ www.kildare.ie/tourism/sites/lullymore; April–Oct Mon–Fri 9am–6pm, Sat & Sun noon–6pm; Nov–March Mon–Fri 9am–4.30pm; individuals €6, family €15.

Set in wooded parkland in the Bog of Allen, the woodland/bog walkways and reconstructions of a Mesolithic campsite with a Neolithic dwelling nearby are fascinating. Children will also enjoy the road train rides, a trip to the little fairy bower, a visit to the café and working off any excess steam at Fionn MacCumhaill's Adventure Park (named after a mythological hero whose reputed birthplace, the Hill of Allen, overlooks the site) – where the attractions include a castle, climbing frames, swings, slides, sand pits, fireman's poles and crazy golf.

## Maynooth Castle

Maynooth, Co. Kildare; ⓣ01/628 6744,
ⓦwww.heritageireland.ie; June–Sept Mon–Fri 10am–6pm, Sat &
Sun 1–6pm; Oct Sun 1–5pm; free, 45min guided tours €1.90;
Heritage card.

A thirteenth-century ruin good for scrambling around and
swashbuckling, this castle contains an exhibition on the occasionally bloodthirsty history of the Fitzgeralds, the Anglo-
Norman dynasty that owned it. Maynooth castle sits next to
the entrance to St Patrick's College, and was one of the family's main strongholds. A massive stone eminence, it kept
Kildare – in fact, most of the rest of Ireland – under
Fitzgerald control until the arrival of the Tudors.

## Straffan Butterfly Farm

Ovidstown, Straffan, Co. Kildare; ⓣ01/627 1109, ⓦwww.kildare-
local.ie; June–Aug daily noon–5.30pm; €6 adult, €4 children,
€16 family.

Three miles southwest of Celbridge (signposted from Kill),
this farm has a tropical greenhouse where butterflies flutter
by freely, while glass tanks safely keep the fiercer-looking
inmates – including an assortment of reptiles, stick insects,
bird-eating spiders, scorpions and tarantulas – away from the
visitors. Those so inclined can satisfy their creepy-crawly pas-
sion, while the butterflies make it a fun and unforgettable
experience for all visitors.

## Millennium Maze, Prosperous

Ballinafagh Farm, Prosperous, Co. Kildare; ⓣ045/861590,
ⓦwww.milleniummaze.com; daily May–Oct noon–6pm; adults
€6, children €4, family €20.

This large 6ft-high hedge maze was grown on Ballinafagh
Farm to mark the Millennium. In the shape of a St Brigid's
Cross, it has over 1.5 miles of paths. There's also an unen-
closed, paved maze, which is a thoughtful added attraction for
younger children, who will appreciate the crazy golf course,
sand pit and pets corner (with ducks, sheep, hens and rabbits)
too. The café and picnic area make a good base for those too
tired to explore.

## Straffan Steam Museum

Straffan, Co. Kildare; ⓣ01/627 3155, ⓦwww.steam-museum.ie;
Easter Sun to May & September Sun and Bank Holidays
2.30–5.30pm, June–Aug Tues-Sun 2–6pm; adults €4, students
€3, children €2, family €13.

Signposted from the N7 road at Kill village, Lodge Park
Heritage Centre's Steam Museum is housed in a Victorian
church. A rose-tinted look back to the good old days of the
industrial revolution, it contains miniature models of steam

trains, locomotives dating from the eighteenth-century and four working steam engines burbling away quietly. The early August holiday weekend brings a steam rally, with even more engines on show, and narrow gauge railway rides set up in the grounds. Refuge from all this engineering may be found in the museum teahouse or in the eighteenth-century walled garden (admission €4 adult, €3 child extra).

# Sport and activities

### Bicycle rental

**Footfalls**, Trooperstown, Roundwood, Co. Wicklow, ☎ 0404/45152, ⓦ www.walkinghikingireland.com; **Johnny Price's Garage**, Main Street, Roundwood, Co. Wicklow, ☎ 01/281 8128; **Hillcrest Hire**, Main Street Blessington, Co. Wicklow, ☎ 045/865066.

### Cinema

**Screen by the Sea**, Victoria Road, Greystones, Co. Wicklow, ☎ 01/287 1143; **Cineplex**, Bray, Co. Wicklow, ☎ 01/286 8686.

### Cycling tours

**Cycling Safaris**, Belfield Bike Shop, University College Dublin, ☎ 01/260 0749, ⓦ www.cyclingsafaris.com; Offers seven-day self-led tours of Wicklow.

### Fishing

**Bray Sports Centre**, 8 Main Street, Bray, Co. Wicklow, ☎ 01/286 3046. Pick up angling permits for the Dargle, and advice on where they might be biting.

### Motor racing

**Mondello Park**, Co. Kildare, ☎ 045/860200, ⓦ www.mondellopark.com; Check for details, although there'll be something exciting going on most weekends from March to October.

### Horseriding

**Co. Wicklow**: Devil's Glen Holiday and Equestrian Village Ashford, ☎ 0404/40637, ⓦ www.devilsglen.ie; Brennanstown Riding School, Hollybrook, Kilmacanogue, Bray, ☎ 01/286 3778, Broomfield Riding School, Broomfield, Tinahely, ☎ 0402/38117; Paulbeg Riding School, Shillelagh, ☎ 055/29100.
**Co. Kildare**: Abbeylands Equestrian Centre, Clane, ☎ 045/868188; Kill International Equestrian Centre, Kill, ☎ 045/877208.

## Water sports and adventure sports

**Blessington Adventure Centre,** Blessington, Co. Wicklow, ⓣ045/865092. Choose between sailing, canoeing, windsurfing, kayaking, tennis, pony trekking, riding and archery.

**The National Mountain and Whitewater Centre**, Devil's Glen Forest, Ashford, Co. Wicklow, ⓣ0404/40169, ⓦwww.tiglin.com; Weekend courses in mountaineering, rock climbing and whitewater kayaking.

# Accommodation

**Roundwood Caravan and Camping Park**, Roundwood, Co. Wicklow; ⓣ01/281 8163. May to mid-Sept; under €13. Facilities include a shop, restaurant and play areas.

**Wicklow Bay Hostel**, Wicklow Town, Co. Wicklow; ⓣ0404/69213; Feb–Nov. Has dorms, four-bed and twin rooms ideal for budget-conscious families. From €15 per person.

**Glendaloch International Hostel**, Co. Wicklow; ⓣ0404/45342. Has private family rooms from €19 and dorms from €14 per person, and bike rental.

**Old Presbytery Hostel**, Rathdrum, Co. Wicklow; ⓣ0404/46930. Comfortable accommodation including dorms at €13 and private family rooms from €16 per person.

**Tynte House**, Dunlavin, Co. Wicklow; ⓣ 045/401561. Good one-to five-bed self-catering apartments and cottages, ideal for families, having a grassy play area, treehouse, games room with table tennis and pool. Bookable by the week at €230–475.

**Kildare Hotel and Country Club**, Straffan, Co. Kildare; ⓣ01/601 7200, ⓦ www.kclub.ie; Luxury hotel with indoor swimming pool, tennis, squash, gym, babysitting. Over €250.

# Places to eat

**Poppies Country Kitchen**, Enniskerry, Co. Wicklow; ⓣ01/282 8869. Homemade lunches (shepherd's pie, quiche, chicken and chips and lasagne, for example), salads, cakes, puddings and teas, open until 6.30pm in summer. Half portions are available.

**The Bakery Restaurant**, Church Street, off Fitzwilliam Square, Wicklow Town; ⓣ0404/66770. A good variety of child-friendly options including ciabatta sandwiches, panini, salads, seafood, pork and rice dishes, all in a pleasant bistro-style setting.

**Kristianna's Bistro**, The Square, Kildare Town; ⓣ045/522985. Specialising in seafood, children can have half portions.

**The Wicklow Heather**, Laragh, Co. Wicklow; ☎ 0404/45157. A popular inn with a moderately priced family restaurant offering steaks, chops and stews.

**Strawberry Tree Restaurant**, at the Brooklodge Hotel Macreddin Village Co. Wicklow; ☎ 0402/36444. Try this restaurant for a top-notch meal made exclusively from organic, free-range and wild ingredients.

# 3

# Laois and Offaly

Comparatively few families holiday in Laois (pronounced "leash") and Offaly, and perhaps that's part of their charm. The landscape of this region between Dublin and the Shannon is seldom breathtaking, yet there are some beautiful areas, notably around the signposted Slieve Bloom Way,

52km/32 miles of tracks through the bog, moorland and pine forest around the Slieve Bloom Mountains.

The main N7 trunk road and main rail line to Limerick cut through the centre of Laois, while the N52 main road straddles Tullamore, the centre of Offaly, and the rail and road hub for the county. Buses from all the major towns pass through Portlaoise, and there are daily services from Dublin to Portumna, and from Cork to Athlone.

## The Abbey Sense Garden

Main Street, Abbeyleix, Co. Laois; ⓣ 0502/31325: May–Sept, daylight hours, free.

The walks through the tranquil sensory gardens of the Brigidine Dove House Convent lead you round the flowerbeds designed to stimulate your senses of vision, smell, touch, taste and sound; on fine days they can give off a combination of smells more potent than a department store perfume counter.

## Stradbally Steam Museum

The Green, Stradbally, Co. Laois; ⓣ 0502/25444, ⓦ www.irish-steam.ie; adults €3, children over 4 €1.

As well as showing a variety of weird and wonderful mechanical exhibits such as ancient fire engines, steam-driven tractors and massive steamrollers, each August the museum hosts The Irish Steam Preservation Society steam-engine rally, which attracts vintage cars too. Call the Portlaoise tourist office for more details.

Stradbally is also home to a Guinness Brewery steam locomotive of 1895 that runs up to Dublin six times each year. The railway is open 2.30–5pm Bank Holiday weekend Sundays and Mondays from Easter to October, and on selected other days in connection with local events; call for details.

## Heywood House Gardens

Ballinakill, Co. Laois; ⓣ 0502/33563, ⓦ www.heritageireland.ie; daily dawn to dusk; free; phone ahead for guided tours.

Little more than a couple of miles southeast of Abbeyleix, children can let off steam on the lawns of these formal gardens. Children appreciate features such as the terraces and little touches like the stone turtles by the fountain.

## Workhouse and Agricultural Museum

Donaghmore, Portlaoise, Co. Laois; ⓣ 0505/46212; May–Sept Mon–Fri 10am–5pm

A visit here gives some idea of the grimmer aspects of the county's history following the great famine of 1845–49. The moving, stimulating, story that unfolds in this harsh building,

which served as the parish workhouse between 1853 and
1886, highlights the extent of rural poverty in the nineteenth
century. The overwhelming size of the establishment indicates
the sheer scale of the problem. Families were frequently broken up on admission and on average two of the 800 inmates
died each week (more ghoulish visitors might be interested
to know that they were buried in a mass grave at the back of
the building).

## Birr Castle and Historic Science Centre

Birr, Co. Offaly, ☎0509/20336, ⓦwww.birrcastle.com; March-Oct
daily 9am-6pm; Nov-Feb 10am-4pm; adults €8, children €4.50,
family €24.

Although much of the castle is still used as a family home,
and so remains closed, but the grounds, with their wild-
flower meadows, artificial lake and a river spanned by a sus-
pension bridge, are beautiful, and open to visitors year-
round. They're the scene of many special events for children including Easter-egg hunts, puppet shows, country
fairs, Hallowe'en parties and Santa visits. The Historic
Science Centre is now home to a collection of optical
equipment that culminates with the 72-inch Great
Telescope, built during the 1840s by the Earl of Rosse, and
the largest in the world at that time.

## Clonmacnois

Shannonbridge, Co. Offaly, ☎090/9674195, ⓦwww.heritageire-
land.ie; Nov to mid-March daily 10am-5.30pm; mid-March to
mid-May 10am-6pm; mid-May to August 9am-7pm; Sept & Oct
10am-6pm; adults €5, children €2, family €11.

Clonmacnois stands out even among the other Celtic sites
crowding the banks of the Shannon, as Ireland's most
important early Christian centre. Located on the banks of
the River Shannon 14 miles from Athlone and signposted
from the main N62 road, the monastic complex founded
here in 548 is now little more than a clutch of ancient
ruins which barely show themselves above the open
ground, dwarfed by a new visitor centre and crowds that
come here. But it was once a huge and important centre of
worship and learning. Having hidden away from the

Vikings and repulsed the Normans, the monastery finally gave way to the English in 1552 and never recovered. Evening visits avoid most of the hubbub and permit quiet reflection on what was a great cauldron of craftsmanship, a royal city and final resting place for the kings of Ireland. Children will have fun charging between the ruined cathedral, the eight ten- to thirteenth-century churches and the two round towers, whilst the adults check out the audio-visual show and café.

## Transport and Heritage Museum

Clonmacnois, Co. Offaly, ☏ 090/6430106; May-Sept daily 10am-5.30pm; adults €4, children €3.

This small museum five miles east of town, just off the main N62 Athlone–Roscrea road, somehow manages to cram in some 1000 exhibits. The collection boasts vintage cars, agricultural vehicles, a threshing mill and other farm machinery, plus a cable car and a very varied collection of bygones including – for no obvious reason – a curiously high number of typewriters and butter churns.

## Clonmacnois and West Offaly Railway

Bord na Mona/The Irish Peat Board, Blackwater Works, Shannonbridge, Co. Offaly; ☏ 090/9674114, ⓦ www.bnm.ie; April-Oct daily 10am-5pm; Nov-March by request only; adults €5, children €3.20, family €14.

This narrow-gauge railway takes you on a 45-minute, 5.5-mile circular guided tour around Blackwater Bog, a 12,000-year-old section of preserved peatlands. Tours leave on the hour after you've seen a video of the history of the bog and its flora and fauna.

## Charleville Forest Castle

Tullamore, Co. Offaly, ☏ 0506/21279; April–May, Sat & Sun 2–5pm; June–Sept Wed–Sun 11am–4pm; Oct–Mar by appointment; minimum €15 for tour for up to three people, then €5 per adult, children 12–18 €4, children 6–11 €4, under 6s free.

You could be forgiven for believing you've been spirited away into a horror film when you set eyes upon this striking limestone Georgian Gothic mansion built in 1779. A classic "mad-scientist" mansion, with towers, spires and turrets, the house also has secret passageways and spooky dungeons with wonderful shaded walks and a grotto on the outside. About ten minutes' walk from the centre of Tullamore, it's just off the Birr road out of town (N52).

# Sport and activities

## Adventure and Activity Centres

**Birr Outdoor Education Centre**, Roscrea Road, Birr, Co. Offaly; ☎0509/20029. The Centre runs courses in kayaking, wind-surfing, rock climbing and so on, and doubles as the Slieve Bloom Interpretive Centre, with information on the region.

## Bike rental

**K. Donegan**, Main Street, Banagher, Co. Offaly, ☎0509/51178; **Laurel Lodge**, Garrymore, Shannonbridge, Co. Offaly, ☎090/9674189; **Racha House**, Shannonbridge, Co. Offaly ☎090/9674249.

## Boat rental

**Laurel Lodge**, Garrymore, Shannonbridge, Co. Offaly; ☎090/9674189. A B&B (€28 per person) that also rents out a boat on the Shannon for four people, €40 per day, free to residents. **Racha House**, Shannonbridge, Co. Offaly; ☎090/9674249. A B&B (€26.50 per person) that also rents out boats; **Shannon Adventure Canoeing Holidays**, The Marina, Banagher, Co. Offaly; ☎0509/51411. Rent a canoe, €40 per day or €15 per first hour, €10 each hour thereafter.

## Cinemas

**Storm Cinema**, Portlaoise, ☎ 050/ 262626; **Dara Cinema**, ☎ 045/897382.

# Accommodation

**The Glebe Caravan and Camping Park**, Clonfanlough, Co. Offaly; ☎0902/30277. Open from Easter–October in a tranquil spot near Clonmacnois. Caravans €10, Car / Tent €6.50 plus €1.50 per person.
**Old Forge**, Banagher, Co. Offaly; ☎0509/51504. This recently renovated two-bedroom house sleeps four, €450 per week.
**Preston House**, Main Street, Abbeyleix, Co. Laois; ☎0502/31432. A comfortable base for the handful of family-friendly attractions nearby. Good quality rooms, €76 per person.
**Roundwood House**, Mountrath, Co. Laois; ☎0502/32120. As well as a friendly welcome in a great base for exploring the Slieve Bloom Mountains, Roundwood offers beautiful parkland containing goats, cows, donkeys, woodland walks and a swing. B&B

costs €60.01 per person; double rooms, all with private bathrooms, are €140

# Places to eat

**Anatolia**, Harbour Street Tullamore, Co. Offaly; ⓣ 0506/23669; closed lunch Sat, dinner Fri & Sat. Mixed international menu; for an exotic change, kids love the Turkish food on offer.

**Kingfisher Indian Restaurant**, Main Street, Portlaoise, Co. Laois; ⓣ 0502/62500. A well-established restaurant, particularly accommodating to families.

**Preston House Restaurant**, Main Street, Abbeyleix, Co. Laois; ⓣ 0502/31432; closed Mon. Good home cooking including scones and home-made preserves and breads, and great vegetarian dishes.

**The Vine House Restaurant and Music Bar**, Banagher, Co. Offaly; ⓣ 0509/51463; restaurant closed Nov-Feb. With a courtyard garden, many dishes are around €10, with kid's half-portions half price. Children's menu (€6.50) includes usual staples like burgers, chicken nuggets and pasta.

# 4

# Meath, Westmeath and Longford

The eastern counties extending from the coast north of Dublin into the heart of the country are perfect for families looking for a rural break. Very different from the west of the country, Meath, Westmeath and Longford are not rich in traditional attractions – although County Meath boasts the largest Norman fortress in Ireland at Trim, and Westmeath's jewels are its lakes. The River Shannon roughly shapes the western border of County Longford, another region of extensive farmland. Its waterways attract families for the boating and other water-based activities.

As for access, a main railway line skirts southern Meath, branching off at Mullingar in the centre of Westmeath to both Longford city and to Athlone, which as the main transport hub of the area, has buses departing for many main towns around the country. The N1, N2, N3, N4 and N6 trunk roads branch out from Dublin like the fingers of a hand, between them covering most areas of the three counties.

## Funtasia

Bettystown, Co. Meath; ⓣ 041/982 8301.
This is a state-of-the-art entertainment centre with a heap of attractions to amuse the whole family, and all under cover. There's a top-notch bowling alley and fully equipped pool and snooker rooms for the older members of the family – while the younger children will have a great time in the multi level play area and disco. Funtasia also has its own indoor fairground with dodgems and other rides, fast food and a licensed restaurant too.

## Brú na Boinne

Donore, Co. Meath; ⓣ 041/988 0300, ⓦ www.heritageireland.ie; June to mid-Sept daily 9am–7pm; Oct–May 9.30am–5pm; combined Newgrange & Knowth tickets: adults €9.50, children €4.50 family, €24.50; Newgrange site only: adults €5.50, children €2.75, family €13.75; Knowth site only: adults €4.25, children €1.50, family €10.50; Visitor Centre: adults €2.75, children €1.50, family €7.
Brú na Boinne, located between Slane and Drogheda on the River Boyne, is one of the most atmospheric ancient sites in the country, guaranteed to enthral young minds through their blending of an unimaginably distant past, impossibly massive boulders and feats of precision engineering. A series of forty or so windswept prehistoric monuments more than 5000 years old, they comfortably predate the Pyramids and Stonehenge and are unmatched anywhere in Europe.

The most important are the three passage graves named Newgrange, Dowth and Knowth – high round mounds raised over stone burial chambers. The scale of the construc-

The East Coast and Midlands Tourism HQ is in Mullingar (☎044/48650) and its website, covering all three counties, is Ⓦwww.ecoast-midlandstourism.ie. Further information is available for Meath from Ⓦwww.meathtourism.ie, and for Longford from the Midlands East Tourism Office, (☎044/48761).

Tourist offices are at Navan, (☎046/9073426); Trim, (☎046/9437111); and Longford (☎043/46566).

tions is stunning: Newgrange, the largest of the trio, looms 36ft tall and is vast, covering more than an acre with a diameter of 260ft. An immense number of giant boulders were somehow heaved up to the site – with one major quartz element coming all the way from the mountains at Wicklow – to be tamped down with what has been estimated as more than a million sacks of smaller stones. Its distinguishing feature is a slitted rock at the entrance, through which a beam of light from the rising sun on the day of the winter solstice enters to illuminate the interior of the tomb. An 18m/60ft passage leads to the burial chamber.

Newgrange is Ireland's most famous prehistoric monument, classed as a World Heritage Site by UNESCO. However, Knowth has only recently opened to the public, and even now just part of the complex may be visited and Dowth remains closed to visitors while excavations continue. The Visitor Centre has a café, along with viewing areas and interpretive displays that make it the best starting-point for seeing the monuments.

## Grove Garden and Tropical Bird Sanctuary

Kells, Co. Meath; ☎046/9434276; mid-March to September daily 10am–6pm; adults €6, children €3.50, family €20.

A very pleasant day out can be had at the Grove, where the tranquil formal gardens, which boast some 400 different roses, amongst other marvels, give way first to the raucous tropical bird garden, where exotic and rare breeds of birds are housed in purpose-built aviaries and then to a mini-zoo that's home to camels, monkeys and racoons.

## Be Irish for a Day!

Causey Farm, Girley, Fordstown, Navan, Co. Meath; ☎046/9434135, Ⓦwww.causeyexperience.com; open by appointment for groups, check for availability for individuals, costs vary.

Don't be put off by the name, this is a great way to spend a day. Something out of the ordinary round of tourist fodder, Causey Farm encourages dirty hands and gently exhausting activities such as treasure hunts, nature trails and modelling with clay. The children can learn how to cut turf, have a bash at hurling, experiment with baking bread, and even dance a jig. Other attractions include working a sheepdog and milking a cow.

## Athlumney Castle

Convent Road, Navan, Co. Meath; no telephone; open to visitors; pick up the keys from Loreto Convent, just before you come to the castle.

Worth the walk of a mile or so from Navan centre, past the bridge and following the signs, this four-storeyed tower house, which dates from the mid-fifteenth century, is now in ruins, and is much more exciting for children than the usual big house on a hillside. There are four floors and turrets to explore, with a secret chamber hidden away down the stairs in the wall on the first floor.

## Loughcrew Gardens

3 miles south of Oldcastle, Co. Meath; ☎049/854 1922, ⓦ www.loughcrew.com; April–Aug daily noon–6pm; Sept–Nov & Jan–March daily noon–4pm; adults €5, children €3, family €15.

Loughgrew's carefully restored gardens include a woodland maze, a watermill cascade and a fairy grotto. The signposted nature and history trails will captivate most younger visitors, while the playground ought to enthral the rest. There's a café for teas, coffees and light meals, or a fine country pub – The Fincourt – up in the village, where seafood is a speciality.

## Slane Castle

Slane, Co. Meath; ☎041/9884400; ⓦ www.slane.ie; mid-May to early-Aug Mon–Thurs & Sun noon–5pm; adult €7, child €4, family €20.

Kids love castles and Slane, set in a 1500-acre estate laid out by Capability Brown, is adorable. It dates from 1785 – although what you see today is mostly the result of restoration and renovation, following an extensive fire in 1992. The

## Tours

There are several tours available from Dublin to Meath's main sites from operators that include Bus Éireann (☎01/836 6111, ⓦ www.buseireann.ie), Gray Line (☎01/676 5377, ⓦ www.gray-line.com) and the very child-friendly Over the Top Tours (best guides in town, reduced prices and free lollipops for kids (☎01/838 6128, ⓦ www.overthetoptours.com). The tourist offices in Dublin can book tickets in advance.

castle boasts an impressive set of battlements and turrets, never intended for real defence, which today has little to keep at bay except the rock fans who engulf the grounds once a year for enormous open-air gigs. Tours take in one of the finest art collections in the country, the main hall, King's Room and ballroom. To finish the visit there's a fine-looking mill across the main road outside the castle, and from Slane village you can walk up the Hill of Slane and scrabble around on the ruined Friary Church. Older children can climb the steep steps of its tower for a great view of the eastern counties.

## Newgrange Farm

Co. Meath; ☎ 041/982 4119; ⓦ www.newgrangefarm.com; May–Aug daily 10am–5pm; €6 per person, €15 family of 3, €5 per person thereafter.

Newgrange is a fun farm, and a delightful place to visit. Feed the ducks, bottle-feed the baby lambs and kid goats (if you visit in spring), see horseshoeing and sheepdog working. At 3pm on Sundays there's a sheep derby, where hapless fleeced runners piloted by teddybear jockeys hurtle around a track, an event that manages to be both exciting and hilarious at the same time.

## Trim Castle

Trim, Co. Meath; ☎ 046/943 8619, ⓦ www.heritageireland.ie; May–Oct daily 10am–6pm; adults €3.50, children €1.25, family €8.25 including 45min guided tour of the keep, from 10.15am and then every 30mins; adults €1.50, children €0.75, family €4.25 excluding the keep. Heritage card.

Trim was used as a location for Mel Gibson's 1995 film *Braveheart*, and is the biggest and most obvious attraction in Trim, although there are numerous other medieval remains in the vicinity. This, the largest Anglo-Norman castle in Ireland, dating back to 1173, dominates the little town even today. Get there early for the tour of the keep as it is very popular. It is safe but a steep climb, and unsuitable for small children.

## Athlone Castle Visitor Centre

St Peter's Square, Athlone, Co. Westmeath; ☎ 090/6472107, ⓦ www.athlone.ie; May–Sept daily 10am–4.30pm; adult €5, child €1.50.

Another castle with a bloody history, the current Norman edifice sits on top of that erected by Tiordelbach, King of Connacht, in 1129. The imposing grey walls now hold nothing more menacing than a visitor centre which documents the gory action seen during the the Siege of Athlone in 1690–91 when 12,000 cannonballs destroyed half the town.

# Glendeer Pet Farm

Athlone, Co. Westmeath; ☎ 090/643 7147, ⓦ www.glendeer.com;
Easter–September Mon–Sat 10am–6pm, Sun noon–6pm,
December Mon–Fri 5-8pm, Sat & Sun 3–8pm; adults €6, children
€5.

Just a few miles west of Athlone, residents at this farm
include deer, Vietnamese pot-bellied pigs, ponies, donkeys,
Jersey cows, sheep, goats and peacocks. There are pet animals to handle, such as puppies, rabbits and guinea pigs, and
an unspoilt nature walk passes historic horse-drawn farm
machinery. As well as a coffee shop, there is a play area with
swings, slides, seesaws and a glider swing and indoor and
outdoor picnic areas.

# Tullynally Castle and Gardens

Castlepollard, Co. Westmeath; ☎ 023/46116; gardens: May–Aug
daily 2–6pm; guided tours of the castle mid–June to end July
daily 2–6pm; gardens: adults €5, children €2; gardens and castle: adults €8, children €4.

Venture through the gatehouse half a mile from
Castlepollard down the road to Granard and you'll find this
beautiful melange of architectural styles based around an
original eighteenth-century tower house. Tullynally Castle
is a masterpiece of landscaped romance set at the end of a
long drive through rolling parkland to the castle itself. The
castle is one of the largest in Ireland, largely Gothic
Revival in style, with four towers and a long series of battlements. The children should find the vast Victorian
kitchen interesting and enjoy the grounds where winding
paths lead to lakes, walled gardens and follies, including a
Chinese garden. There are tree carvings to look out for and
a treasure trail to follow before hitting the café for tea, coffee and home-made cakes.

# Belvedere House, Gardens and Park

Tullamore Road, Mullingar, Co. Westmeath; ☎ 044/49060,
ⓦ www.belvedere-house.ie; May–Aug Mon–Fri 9.30am–6pm,
Sat & Sun 10.30am–7pm, Sept & Oct daily 10.30am–6pm,
Nov-April daily 10.30am–4.30pm; adults €6, children €3.80,
family €16

Three miles from Mullingar on the N52 road, this elegant
hunting and fishing lodge dates from 1740, and its grounds
are beautiful; terraces run down to a lake, there are woodlands, a walled garden, an ice house and stables to explore.
More modern resources on site include a children's play area,
animal sanctuary, tram (open certain days only, adults €1.50,
children €1) and coffee shop. The visitor's centre features a
multimedia presentation about the history of the estate and
its restoration.

## Viking Tours

7 St Mary's Place, Athlone, Co. Westmeath; ☎ 090/6473383,
ⓦ www.iol.ie/wmeathtc/viking/; May–Sept.

A fine and inventive way to get the kids to join you on a tour
out to Lough Ree (afternoon trips from 1pm) or to
Clonmacnois (a 4hr trip departing 9am); you travel in a replica
longboat and the young ones get to dress up as Vikings. Prior
booking is essential and ticket costs vary depending upon group
size.

## Corlea Trackway Visitor Centre

Kenagh, Co. Longford; ☎ 043/22386, ⓦ www.heritageireland.ie;
April–Sept, 10am–6pm; adults €3.50, children €1.25, family
€8.25, Three miles or so from Kenagh Village, just off the
Kenagh–Longford R397 road. Heritage Card.

Anyone who finds fascination in the ancient past will relish the
Corlea trackway, a stretch of oak-built, Iron Age bog road built
in 148 BC – the largest of its type uncovered in Europe. The
visitor centre maintains the excavated 60ft of the path in air-
conditioned comfort and places it in context using informative
displays on life in the boglands two thousand years ago, a video
presentation and informative guided tours that venture outside
into the bog of today.

## Carrigglas Manor

Lefroy, Co. Longford; ☎ 043/48135, ⓦ www.carrigglass.com;
May–Sept Mon, Tues, Fri & Sat 11am–3pm; Adult €9, Children
€6, group rates available. Gardens and museum only €5

Adults and older children will enjoy the refined splendour of
this handsome, imposing Gothic Revival castle built in 1837. It's
set in grounds with a formal water garden fed by a stream (and
more recently added woodland walks to entertain the younger
kids). The Manor House is one of only sixty Irish great houses
still owned by the original family and is still very obviously used
as a home. Tours take in the ornately plastered dining room,
drawing room and library, and there's a costume and lace museum to round off the visit, with a collection dating mainly from
the mid-eighteenth century.

# Sports and activities

## Boat cruises

**Athlone Cruisers**, Jolly Mariner Marina, Athlone; ☎
090/6472892, ⓦ www.iol.ie/wmeathtc/acl. Ninety-minute Lough
Ree cruises May-Sept. Also rents out cabin cruisers.

## Horseriding

**Kells Equestrian Centre**, Kells, Co. Longford, ⓣ 046/924 6638.
**Moy Riding Centre**, Summerhill, ⓣ 046/955 7575.

# Accommodation

**The Fincourt**, Oldcastle, Co. Meath; ⓣ 049/854 1153,
ⓦ www.fincourt.com; This pub also offers tasteful B&B and self-contained apartment accommodation from €30 per person.
**Kells Hostel**, Kells, Co. Meath; ⓣ 046/9249995. Hostel with 4-bed, 6-bed and 8-bed family rooms, for €14-18 per person – and its own pub.
**Longford Arms**, Main Street Longford, Co. Longford,
ⓣ 043/46296, ⓦ www.longfordarms.ie; Comfortable accommodation, leisure centre with pool and gym, restaurant and coffee shop. €70 per adult, €15 children B&B.
**Newgrange Hotel**, Bridge Street Navan, Co. Meath;
ⓣ 046/9074100, ⓦ www.newgrangehotel.ie An upmarket option, with a good restaurant and babysitting available. Doubles €135, children €30 supplement, under 5s free.

# Places to eat

**Aubergine Gallery Café**, 1 Ballymahon Street, Longford, Co. Longford; ⓣ 043 48633. Lunch: Tues–Sun 12–3; Dinner: Wed–Sat 6–9.30 in winter, Tues–Sat in Summer. Contemporary dishes like aubergine, feta and olive bruschetta can be half-portions and there are kid-friendly options like chicken or sausage and chips.
**Boyle's Tea Rooms**, Main Street, Slane, Co. Meath;
ⓣ 041/9824195. Fully licensed and with a range of inexpensive but delicious homemade food.
**Gallery 29 Café**, Oliver Plunkett Street, Mullingar, Co. Westmeath; ⓣ 044/49449. Good, inventive café specialising in seasonal specialities in the organic/free-range line.
**The Loft**. Main Street, Kilbeggan Co. Westmeath; ⓣ 0506 32243. Simple, good-value dishes like baked potato, quiche and salads in an inviting café.
**Woodville House**, Gaybrook, Mullingar, Co. Westmeath;
ⓣ 044/43694. Country cooking with half portions half price, cken and chips €8.

# 5

# Louth, Monaghan and Cavan

The border counties of Louth, Monaghan and Cavan are three of the least visited by families holidaying in Ireland, but each certainly has attractions well worth seeing.

Louth is the Republic's smallest county and much of its everyday activity is focused upon the towns of Drogheda and Dundalk. Apart from the small resort of Clogherhead, its coastline is largely undeveloped, though Carlingford, on the Cooley peninsula, is rapidly becoming a very popular holiday spot, thanks to its position overlooking Carlingford Lough and its surrounding good walking countryside. The county also has several important monastic and prehistoric sites.

County Monaghan consists mainly of gently rolling countryside, a mix of rounded hills known as drumlins and tiny lakes, with facilities dotted around or in the towns of Monaghan itself, Castleblayney, Carrickmacross and Clones. Cavan is known for its multitude of lakes and the opportunities offered for boating and angling, as well as fine walking in the west of the county. Its only sizeable centre of population is Cavan town itself, though Ballyconnell, Ballyjamesduff and Belturbet are all pleasant enough in their own right.

All three counties are ideal cycling country. Indeed both Cavan and Monaghan are part of the 230-mile Kingfisher Trail, while the Táin Trail meanders through Louth (℡042/933 5484 for details).

## Millmount Museum

Millmount, Drogheda, Co. Louth; ℡041/983 3097, Ⓦwww.millmount.net; Mon–Sat 10.30am–6pm, Sun 2.30–5.30, adults €5.50, children €3, family €12.

The museum sits at the top of Millmount hill, south of the river Boyne, and provides a superb view of Drogheda town set out below. The Martello tower here dates from Napoleonic times, but was seriously damaged in 1922 during

### Information

For details of local events and attractions in County Louth visit Ⓦwww.ecoast-midlands.travel.ie or wwww.louthholidays.com. Information about the Drogheda area is also available at Ⓦwww.drogheda-tourism.com and for the Cooley peninsula at Ⓦwww.carlingford.ie. Tourist offices can be found at Carlingford, ℡042/937 3033; Drogheda, two offices – ℡041/983 7070 & ℡041/984 5684; and Dundalk, ℡042/933 5484.

Details of events in Co. Cavan can be found at Ⓦwww.cavantourism.com and the county's sole tourist office is in Cavan town, ℡049/433 1942. Visit Ⓦwww.monaghantourism.com for similar information about Co. Monaghan whose only tourist office is in Monaghan town, ℡047/81122.

the Irish Civil War. The collection comprises material on the town's history, especially its industries, and includes such exhibits as a Boyne coracle - a circular boat made from a framework of hazel twigs and the hide of a prize bull - and a nineteenth-century period kitchen complete with fittings and fixtures.

## Louth County Museum

Jocelyn St, Dundalk, Co. Louth; ☎ 042/932 7056, ⓦ www/heritageisland.com/attractions/dundalkmuseum.html. Mon–Sat 10.30am–5.30pm, Sun 2–6pm except Oct–April closed Mon; adults €3.80, children €1.25, family €10.15.

In addition to hosting summer concerts and staging regular temporary exhibitions, the County Museum traces the history of Dundalk and surrounding area from prehistoric times to the present day, using a variety of formats, including computerized interactive displays. Of greatest interest to children will be the Heinkel bubble car, dating from 1966; using the cockpit from the German Heinkel bomber plane these were transformed into three-wheeled vehicles in Dundalk during the 1960s.

## Proleek Dolmen

Dundalk, Co. Louth; open access.

Accessed via the car park of the Ballymascanlon Hotel (three miles from Dundalk down the R173 Carlingford road) and near the fifth green of its golf course, the Proleek Dolmen is one of the most photographed prehistoric monuments in Ireland. Its huge 46-ton capstone seems to balance rather dangerously on three upright supports, but the monument's endurance is proof of its real solidity. One local belief is that, if you can throw a stone and make it land on the top, a wish will be granted. Another says that the gallery grave also here is that of a giant who came from Scotland to challenge the legendary Finn McCool and came to a sticky end.

## Stephenstown Pond, Agnes Burns Cottage and Visitor Centre

Knockbridge, Dundalk, Co. Louth; ☎ 042/937 9019, ⓦ www.stephenstownpond.com; Stephenstown Pond Nature Park: daily May–Sept 8.30am–8.30pm, Oct–April 10am–5pm; free. Cottage and Visitor Centre: daily May–Sept 9.30am–5pm, Oct–April 10am–3pm; €2 per person.

The result of a community-led initiative, this five-acre site encompasses pleasant woodland, waterside walks and a pond stocked with carp (fishing permits available from the visitor centre). A cottage in the grounds was the home of Agnes Burns, sister of the Scottish poet Robert Burns, and it was her husband, William Galt, who was contracted to construct the during the early nineteenth century. The cottage has been restored in period style and contains information on both Robert and Agnes Burns and the latter's working life. The visitor centre includes an interactive display on Louth's wildlife and a coffee shop as well as a multimedia room providing internet access.

## Knockabbey Castle and Gardens

Knockabbey, Louth village, Co. Louth; ℡01/677 8816, Ⓦwww.knockabbeycastle.com; May–Sept Tues–Sun 10.30am–5.30pm; house – adults €5, children €3, family €15; gardens – adults €5, children €3, family €15; combined – adults €9, children €6, family €25.

Children are more likely to enjoy the attractive gardens and the treasure trail (which can be downloaded in advance from the Castle's website) than Knockabbey itself, although there's a small interpretative centre which explains much of the house's history as well as the development and restoration of its gardens. These form the real pleasure of the visit and a stroll through their mixture of Victorian flower gardens and medieval water gardens, alongside buildings such as a pergola and a gazebo, is delightful in sunny weather.

## Monasterboice Round Tower and High Crosses

Monasterboice, Co. Louth; open access.

If you're travelling northwards along the N1 from Drogheda, look out for the signs to Monasterboice, about six miles on the way. In the midst of an old graveyard, situated in a tranquil, sylvan location, stands one of the tallest round towers in Ireland. Rising to a height of 110 feet, its door was originally some fifteen to twenty feet above the ground and reached by wooden steps, but the entrance has sunk to ground level over the ten centuries or so since the tower was constructed. Unfortunately, you cannot enter the tower for safety reasons. The other major attraction here is a pair of splendid high crosses, carved with all manner of decorations depicting parts of the Bible. Part of the fun in visiting is to try and decipher their meaning; fortunately, there's an information panel available to guide you.

## Irish Country Quads

Carrickakelly, Inniskeen, Co. Monaghan; ℡042/ 937 8997; opening times by arrangement; adults €35 per hour, children €28 per hour.

Older children will thoroughly relish the chance to drive a four-wheeled ATV (All Terrain Vehicle) around the Monaghan countryside. Courses are designed to cater for individual ability and experience and include such thrills as an underground tunnel, various water splashes, tight corners, rugged ground and muddy ditches. Waterproof clothing, boots, gloves and helmets are all provided.

## Killykeen Forest Park

Killykeen, Co. Cavan; ☎ 049/433 2541; dawn–dusk; free.

Some five miles west of Cavan town off the Killeshandra road, Killykeen Forest Park has plenty of woodland trails and contains historical sites such as the ruined Clogh Oughter Castle. The park is set around the shores of the many intertwining little lakes which actually form the southernmost reach of Upper Lough Erne. There's also a children's play area, tennis courts, boat and bike hire, an equestrian centre and log cabin accommodation (for both see below).

# Sports and activities

## Activity and adventure centres

**Co. Louth**: **Carlingford Adventure Centre**, Tholsel St, Carlingford, ☎ 042/937 3100, Ⓦ www.carlingfordadventure.com; **East Coast Adventure**, Marina, Carlingford, ☎ 042/937 3118, Ⓦ www.eastcoastadventure.com; **Neptune Adventure Centre**, Clogherhead, ☎ 041/983 4422; and **Tain Holiday Village**, Ballyoonan, Omeath, ☎ 042/937 5385, Ⓦ www.tainvillage.com. **Co. Monaghan**: **Muckno Adventure Centre**, Lough Muckno Park, Castleblayney, ☎ 086/3131612; **Tanagh Outdoor Education Centre**, Dartrey Forest, Rockcorry, ☎ 049/555 2988.

## Bike rental

**McQuaid Cycle Hire**, Glaslough, Co. Monaghan, ☎ 047/88108; **Quay Cycles**, 11a North Quay, Drogheda, Co. Louth, ☎ 041/983 4526; **Snipe Cycle Hire**, Clones, Co. Monaghan, ☎ 047/52125.

## Cinemas

**The Diamond Screen Cinema**, The Diamond, Monaghan town, Co. Monaghan, ☎ 047/84755; **IMC Cinema**, Cassore Village, Longwalk, Dundalk , Co. Louth, ☎ 042/34843; **Omniplex**, Abbey Shopping Centre and Boyne Shopping Centre, Drogheda, Co. Louth, ☎ 041/984 4007, Ⓦ www.filminfo.net; **Storm Cinemas**, Main St Car Park, Cavan town, Co. Cavan, ☎ 049/437 2005.

## Go-karting

**Speedway Kart Racing**, Dublin Rd, Cavan town, Co. Cavan; ☎ 049/437 3549.

## Horseriding

**Co. Cavan**: **Ashfield Riding Stables**, Ashfield, Cootehill, Co. Cavan, ℡ 049/555 2045; **Cavan Equestrian Centre**, Shalom Stables, Latt , ℡ 4049/32017; **Killykeen Equestrian Centre**, Killykeen Forest Park, ℡ 049/61707; **Lough Sheelin Equestrian Centre**, Ross House Mountnugent, Co. Cavan, ℡ 049/854 2018; **Redhills Equestrian Centre**, Killymare, Redhills, Co. Cavan, ℡ 047/952 6121.

**Co. Louth**: **Beltichburn Equestrian Centre**, Termonfeckin Rd, Drogheda, ℡ 041/983 8063; **Ravensdale Lodge Equestrian and Trekking Centre**, Ravensdale, Dundalk, ℡ 042/937 1034, Ⓦ www.ravensdalelodge.com.

**Co. Monaghan**: **Carrickmacross School of Equitation,** Drumconrath Rd, Carrickmacross, ℡ 042/ 9661017; **Greystones Equestrian Centre**, Glaslough, ℡ 047/88100, Ⓦ www.grey-stones-ireland.com; **Mullaghmore Equestrian Centre**, Mullaghmore, Tydavnet, ℡ 047/89645.

## Pitch and putt

**Co. Cavan**: **Ballyhaise Pitch and Putt**, Ballyhaise, ℡ 049/38430.
**Co. Louth**: **Boyne Valley Hotel**, Stameen, Dublin Rd, Drogheda, ℡ 041/984 3280; **Cement Pitch and Putt**, Cement Rd, Drogheda, ℡ 041 983 03050; **Channonrock Pitch and Putt Club**, nr. Louth village, ℡ 042/937 4117; **Collon Pitch and Putt Club**, Collon, ℡ 041/982 6139; **McBride Pitch and Putt Club**, Weirhope, Drogheda, ℡ 086/838 5713; and **Seapoint Pitch and Putt Club**, Termonfeckin, ℡ 041/988 1315.
**Co. Monaghan**: **Inniskeen Pitch and Putt**, Inniskeen, ℡ 042/937 8230; **Lakeview Pitch and Putt Club**, Ardee Rd, Carrickmacross, ℡ 042/966 4269; **Malone's Pitch and Putt Club**; Muldrummond, Castleblayney, ℡ 042/974 0613; **Monaghan Valley Pitch and Putt**, Killygowan, Monaghan town, ℡ 047/84928; **Rowan Springs Pitch and Putt**, Doohamlet, Castleblayney, ℡ 042/974 1278.

## Swimming

**Bailieborough Swimming & Leisure Centre**, Chapel Road, Bailieborough, Co. Cavan; ℡ 042/966 6644.

## Ten-pin bowling

**Astra Bowl**, Storm Cinema Complex, Townspark, Cavan town, Co. Cavan, ℡ 049/437 2662, Ⓦ www.astra-bowl.com; **Blayney Bowls**, Monaghan Rd, Castleblayney, Co. Monaghan, ℡ 042/974 9944, Ⓦ www.blayney-bowl.com.

## Water-skiing

**Lough Muckno Waterski Club**, Lough Muckno Park, Castleblayney, Co. Monaghan; ☏087/666 0077, Ⓦwww.skimuckno.com.

# Accommodation

**Boyne Valley Hotel and Country Club**, Stameen, Dublin Road, Drogheda, Co. Louth; ☏041/983 7737, Ⓦwww.boyne-valley-hotel.ie/accomodation.html. Set in expansive landscaped gardens, southeast of Drogheda on the N1, the hotel has its own swimming pool and pitch and putt course; from €79 per person per night with children under-6 at €21.50 and 6–12s at €32. Special midweek deals available.

**The Glencarn Hotel and Leisure Centre**, Monaghan Rd, Castleblayney, Co. Monaghan; ☏042/974 6666. This very family-friendly hotel not only has a children's swimming pool, but a gym too and offers a babysitting service; family rooms start at €126 plus around €25–30 for each child.

**Killykeen Forest Chalets**, Killykeen Forest Park, Co. Cavan; ☏049/433 2541, Ⓦwww.coillte.ie/tourism_and_recreation/killykeen_forest_hols.htm. Self-catering Scandinavian-style chalets or log cabins in a tranquil spot; prices for a two-bedroom cabin are €245–500 per week and for a three-bed €255–600.

**The Lennard Arms**, The Diamond, Clones, Co. Monaghan; ☏047/51075. Very friendly hotel, offering large rooms, (some with two double beds) from €40 per person with reductions for children; the downstairs bar also serves splendid meals and has an above average children's menu.

**Riverside Farmhouse**, off Cavan Road, Cootehill, Co. Cavan; ☏049/555 2150. Very pleasant Victorian house with riverside views with a family room, a triple and three doubles; from €25 per person with a 20% reduction for children.

**Shalom**, Ghan Rd, Carlingford, Co. Louth; ☏042/937 3151, Ⓦwww.jackiewoods.com; Well-equipped B&B by the side of the lake with prices from €27 per person and offering a fifty percent reduction for children.

# Places to eat

**Andy's Bar and Restaurant**, 12 Market St, Monaghan town; ☏047/82277. Hearty lunches and a more exotic evening menu. Bayleaf Café, Main St, Ballyconnell. Extremely good value café and takeaway, open in the evenings too.

**Hope Castle**, Lough Muckno Park, Castleblayney, Co. Monaghan; ℡ 042/974 9450. Fine bar meals and plenty of options in the restaurant too.

**The Oystercatcher Bistro**, Market Square, Carlingford, Co. Louth; ℡ 042/937 3922. Serves a variety of seafood and meat dishes.

**La Pizzeria**, Peter St, Drogheda, Co. Louth; ℡ 041/983 4208. Exceptionally popular pizza parlour.

# 6

# Wexford, Carlow and Kilkenny

This part of Ireland may not possess huge expanses of bog-land, rock and water, but it does have plenty of outstandingly beautiful countryside to entertain family visitors. It also has the advantage of being Ireland's sunniest and driest cor-ner. The landscape is perhaps at its most attractive amongst the valleys and hills of the Rivers Nore and Barrow, just north of New Ross and south of Kilkenny city, and ideal for walking and cycling. Walkers will also love the mountains, valleys and open farmland of the South Leinster Way and the Wexford Coastal Path.

Public transport isn't exceptional, although you can travel to a surprisingly large number of the attractions in the area (the exception being Carlow) by train: the line slices through County Wexford to Wexford City and Rosslare, then contin-ues to New Ross and Kilkenny City via Waterford.

## Ballyhack Castle and Dunbrody Abbey

Ballyhack, Co. Wexford; ℡ 051/389468,
Ⓦ www.heritageireland.ie; June–Sept daily Mon–Fri 10am–1pm, 2–6pm, Sat & Sun 10am–6pm; adults €1.30, €0.50 children, €4 family. Heritage Card.

Set in picturesque surroundings, this stoutly proportioned five-storey, sixteenth-century tower house makes an ideal starting-point for a family exploration of the area. The castle tower can be climbed to about halfway up its full height, helping build an appetite for the offerings of the rather upmarket seafood restaurant, *The Neptune*, while just to the northeast off the R733 is the ruin of Dunbrody Abbey (April–June & Sept daily 10am–6pm, July & Aug 10am–7pm; €1.90), which dates from the thirteenth century and makes for a pleasant, post-lunch stroll. There's a handy car ferry from Ballyhack village that'll run Waterford-based visitors back to the village of Passage East across the harbour. Trips take just 10 minutes (℡ 051/382190, €6.50 single, €9.50 return).

## Enniscorthy Castle and Wexford County Museum

Castle Hill, Enniscorthy; ℡ 054/35926; June–Sept daily 10am–6pm, Oct–Nov & Feb–May daily 2–5.30pm, Dec & Jan Sun 2–5pm; adults €4.50, children €1, family €11.

At the top of Castle Hill overlooking the River Slaney, this formidable, well-preserved and restored Norman castle con-tains the Wexford County Museum, which has separate rooms displaying different aspects of the region, such as its seafaring, agricultural, industrial, military and ecclesiastical past. There's anything from a mammoth's tooth to black-smith's tools and 150-year-old sewing machines, and plenty of pikes, bayonets, swords and muskets in the 1798 Room to keep the most military-mad youngster happy. There is an old

Irish farm kitchen and a display about early forms of travel as well as old gramophones, a coin collection and even a set of African artifacts. The castle itself has had a colourful history: it served as a prison after the 1798 Rebellion, and a picture of a soldier scratched on a dungeon wall by an imprisoned rebel can still be seen.

## National 1798 Visitor Centre

Millpark Road, Enniscorthy, Co. Wexford; ⓣ 054/37596, ⓦ www.1798centre.com; Mon–Sat 9.30am–5pm, Sun 11am–5pm; adults €5.

The dramas of the 1798 Rebellion are brought vividly to life at this excellent visitor centre, opened in 1998 to mark the bicentenary of this key event in Irish history, where disorganized rebels around the country, against a background of French Revolution and independence in America, were suppressed at a cost of over 30,000 lives and which changed the course of Irish history. Audiovisual and interactive exhibits help explain the complicated issues that led up to the insurrection.

## Hook Lighthouse, Hook Head Peninsula

Fethard-on-Sea, Co. Wexford; ⓣ 051/397055, ⓦ www.thehook-wexford.com; March–Oct daily 9.30am–5.30pm, Nov–Feb contact centre for opening times; adults €4.75, children €2.75, family €14.

The bracing Hook Head Peninsula has plenty of isolated spots for picnics, including good sandy beaches, such as Booley Strand, two miles to the south of Duncannon. Junior naturalists will enjoy watching the thousands of migrating birds that rest here and may be lucky enough to spot the seals which can sometimes be seen. The beaches are mostly unsuitable for swimming – the currents here make it dangerous for enough for boats, and the tip of the peninsula is the site of Europe's oldest lighthouse – the first having been built here in the twelfth century.

# Guillemot Maritime Museum

Co. Wexford; ☎ 051/561144; May–Sept daily noon–6pm; April &
Oct Sat & Sun noon–6pm; adult e4, child e2, family e10.

Exhibits evoke the tough life at sea and are housed in an old
120ft long, 30ft wide lightship built in 1922 embedded
around concrete alongside the marina at this small, attractive
fishing and holiday village of thatched cottages, whitewashed
walls, ice-cream parlours, cafés, restaurants, craftshops and a
sandy beach. Children can explore the three levels of the boat,
seeing the sailor's cabins, captain's all-mahogany room and the
engine room. There are ships in bottles, models of boats made
by local sailors going back to 1880 and coral from the sea.

# Ballylane Visitor Farm

Co. Wexford; Signposted off the N25 road three miles east of
New Ross; ☎051/425666, ⓦwww.southeastireland.com/bally-
lanefarm; April, noon–6pm Sundays only; May–Sept, daily
10am–6pm; Oct–Mar, Sundays only, noon–6pm; adults €5, children €3, family €15.

This working family farm offers a rare insight into farm life.
Very much more than just another petting zoo, Ballylane
offers friendly and informative tours that illustrate sheep,
pheasant and deer husbandry, and tillage, passing through
woodland, bogland and a nature reserve. The tearoom, shop,
play and picnic areas offer the traditional end to a visit.

# Dunbrody Emigrant Ship

South Quay, New Ross; Co. Wexford; ☎ 051/425239;
ⓦwww.dunbrody.com; April–Sept daily 9am–6pm, Oct–March
10am–5pm; adults €6.50, children €4, family €18.

Starting-out seafarers can test the waters on this magnificent
authentic replica of an 1845 three-masted, 458ton, 176ft-long
famine ship, which would have crossed the Atlantic crammed
with those escaping Ireland's Great Famine. Audiovisual and
interactive displays help to bring the subject of emigration to
life, and children get to meet the captain, crew and some of
the emigrants telling their stories.

# Duncannon Fort Visitor Centre

New Ross, Co. Wexford; ☎ 051/389454; April to mid-Sept
10am–5.30pm; adults €4, children €2; family €10.

This huge star-shaped fortress built in 1584 in anticipation of
invasion by the Spanish Armada is a hit with kids, who can
climb the ramparts for great views of the harbour. In the
summer there are occasional re-enactments of battles and
there's a maritime museum explaining the origins of the fishing village of Duncannon. It contains pieces of shipwrecks
and several model boats.

# Irish National Heritage Park

☎ 053/20733; Ⓦ www.inhp.com; March–Oct daily
9.30am–6.30pm, closing times may vary; adults €7, children
4–12 €3.50, 13–16 year-olds €4, family €17.50.

Close to the mouth of the Slaney at Ferricarrig, this park
presents nine thousand years of Irish history using full-scale
models of settlements, homesteads, a medieval tower and burial places. Children especially will adore the Mesolithic
campsite and Viking shipyard, both brought to life by costumed interpreters.

## Irish Agricultural Museum

Johnstown Castle, Bridgetown Road, Wexford; ☎ 053/42888;
gardens: daily 9.30am–5.30pm; museum: April, May, Sept & Oct
Mon–Fri 9am–12.30pm & 1.30–5pm, Sat & Sun 2–5pm;
June–Aug Mon–Fri 9am–5pm, Sat & Sun 11am–5pm; Nov–March
Mon–Fri 9am–12.30pm & 1.30–5pm; museum: adults €3, chil-
dren €2, family €10; gardens: adults €2, children €0.70, car €4.

The trades of Ireland's past are brought graphically to life by
the replica workshops of a blacksmith, wheelwright, cooper,
basket-maker and harness maker. Other child-friendly displays, set in old farm buildings, bring rural ways back to life,
and include a travellers' caravan, carriages and machinery. The
museum is set in the gardens ofJohnstownCastle, a neo-
Gothic mansion, and children can explore the grounds (May-
Oct) which contain ornamental lakes, hothouses, a statue
walk, dark woodlands and walled gardens.

## North Slobs Wildfowl Reserve

☎ 053/23129; daily April–Sept 9am–6pm, Oct–March 10am–5pm;
free.

This wildlife reserve, located at the splendidly named "North
Slobs" mudflats, is a magnet for twitchers of all ages. Between
October and April they come to see the huge number of
migrating birds, notably white-fronted geese from Greenland.
The visitor centre provides excellent preparation for viewing
wildfowl on the reserve, which is well furnished with hides
and lookout towers. The reserve is signposted off the Gorey
road (R741) north out of Wexford.

## Dunmore Cave

Castlecomber Road, Ballyfoyle, Co. Kilkenny; ☎ 056/776 7726;
mid-March to mid-June & mid-Sept to Oct daily 10am–5pm; mid-
June to mid-Sept daily 10am–7pm; Nov–mid-March, Sat, Sun &
public holidays 10am–5pm; €2.50

This cave is seven miles north of Kilkenny (the N77 road and
then the N78) on an isolated limestone outcrop of the
Castlecomer plateau; kids love the experience of climbing the

many steps down into the stalagmite and stalactite-ridden cave, which is a bit like living in a black and white 1950s science fiction film. In 928AD it was thought to be the site of a Viking massacre. Although Ireland has larger caves to visit, Dunmore is well lit and easily accessed. The sleek and modern visitor centre by the cave has several displays and there is an excellent introductory film that, despite explaining in depth how the cave was formed, manages to captivate even the youngest viewers.

### Kilkenny Castle grounds

The Parade, Kilkenny; ☎056/772 1450.
While the tours of the castle itself largely focus on fine art, children are likely to be more interested in the gardens and parkland, which include a playground and riverside walk.

### Nore Valley Park Open Farm

Bennettsbridge, Co. Kilkenny; ☎056/7727229, ⓦnorevalley-park.tripod.com/farm/; April–Sept, Mon–Sat, 9am–8pm; €3.80
This is a great day out for the family because, as well as plenty of animals there is a straw-covered playing area, a playground with swings and slides as well as pedal go-karts (extra €1.50), crazy golf (extra €2.50) and trailer rides (extra €0.50). Children are encouraged to feed the animals and can view them from an American-style fort in the grounds.

# Sport and activities

### Bicycle rental

**Co. Wexford**: Arthurstown Youth Hostel, Arthurstown, ☎051/389411; The Bike Shop, 9 Selskar Street, Wexford, ☎053/22514; Kenny's Bike, Slaney Street, Enniscorthy, ☎054/33255; Kilmore Quay Bike Hire, Island View House Kilmore Quay, ☎053/29781.
**Co. Carlow**: Celtic Cycling Bagenalstown, ☎0503/75282; A.E. Coleman, 19 Dublin Street, Carlow, ☎0503/31273.
**Co. Kilkenny**: J.J. Wall, Maudlin Street, Kilkenny, ☎056/772 1236.

### Boat rental and cruises

**Dick Hayes**, Kilmore Quay, Co. Wexford; ☎053/29704, ☎Mobile 0872 549111. Mr Hayes and his boat can be hired for €350 per six-hour day for up to ten people, individuals (adults and children both cost €50), based on availability, and from June–Sept hiring the boat for €150 for three-hour evening trips is popular with families.

**Galley Cruising Restaurant**, New Ross, Co. Wexford; ☎051/421723. Boat trips run from Easter to October up the Barrow and Nore.

**Valley Boats**, Graiguenamanagh, Co. Kilkenny; ☎0503/9724945. Barges and narrow boats for hire by the week, from €700–1400 depending upon size and time of year.

**Wexford Harbour Trips**. Trips around Wexford Harbour cost €7 per person and run throughout the summer. Book through Kirwan House Hostel, 3 Mary Street, Wexford; ☎053/21208.

## Horseriding

**Boro Hill Equestrian Centre**, Clonroche, Co. Wexford ☎054/44117; **Horetown House** Foulksmills, Co. Wexford ☎051/565771; **Seaview Trekking Centre**, Hook Head, Co. Wexford ☎051/562239; **Shelmalier Riding Stables**, Wexford (☎053/39251).

## Leisure Centres

**Forest Park Leisure Centre**, Courtown, Gorey, Co. Wexford; ☎055/24849. Three swimming pools and water slide.

## Quad biking

**Country Quads**, Tinnecarrig Borris Co. Carlow, ☎059/972 4624; **Quad Attack**, Clonroche Enniscorthy, Co. Wexford, ☎054/44660.

# Accommodation

**Hibernian Hotel**, 1 Ormonde Street, Kilkenny; ☎056/777 1888, ⓦwww.kilkennyhibernianhotel.com; Upmarket hotel €200–250) with leisure centre and pool for rainy days.

**Kelly's Resort Hotel**, Rosslare, Co. Wexford; ☎53/32114, ⓦwww.kellys.ie; A hotel that especially welcomes families with excellent sporting facilities including a pool, indoor tennis and squash as well as miniature golf and a playground. €130–160.

**St Margaret's Beach Caravan and Camping Park**; Rosslare, Co. Wexford; ☎053/31169. Close to the beach and particularly welcoming families. Pitch rate for a family tent €13–18.

**Talbot Hotel**, Trinity Street, Wexford; ☎053/22566, ⓦwww.talbothotel.ie. Pleasant family-orientated three-star hotel with leisure centre, swimming pool and babysitting facilities. €90–160.

# Places to eat

**Antique Tavern**, Enniscorthy, Co. Wexford; ☎054/33428. On the quayside, this popular pub decorated with Wexford memorabilia including mounted elk heads and a glass case containing money from around the world offers simple meals like sandwiches and soups.

**Cappuccino's**, 23 North Main Street, Wexford; ☎053/22311. Good-value Mediterranean snacks, burgers and baguettes.

**M.L. Dore**, 65 High Street, Kilkenny. Well-established cafe with inexpensive snacks, sandwiches, cakes etc.

**Into The Blue**, 80 South Main Street, Wexford; ☎053/22011. Inexpensive snack bar and restaurant with generous sandwiches and bagettes (€4), fajitas and paninis (€6) and children's portions available on dishes like pasta or curry (€9.50).

**Italian Connection**, Parliament Street, Kilkenny; ☎056/64225. Good Italian food like kiddies' favourites pizza and pasta in a convivial, if a little dark, atmosphere.

**Key Largo,** Canal Street, Kilkenny; ☎056/23922. Inexpensive, with vegetarian dishes, pasta, pizza, salads, fajitas.

**Lennon's Café Bar**, 121 Tullow Street, Carlow. Prize-winning and stylish gastropub.

# 7

# Waterford, Tipperary and Limerick

**Co. Waterford**: Dungarvan, ⓣ058/41741; Lismore, ⓣ058/54975; Waterford Town, ⓣ051/875823.
**Co. Tipperary**: Cahir, ⓣ052/41453 (April–Sept); Carrick-on-Suir, ⓣ051/640200; Cashel, ⓣ062/61333 (May–Sept); Clonmel, ⓣ052/26500; Nenagh, ⓣ067/31610 (mid-May–mid-Sept); Tipperary Town, ⓣ062/33466 (May–Sept).
**Co. Limerick**: Adare, ⓣ061/396255, (June–Sept); Limerick Town, ⓣ061/317522.

These three counties are ideal for a restful rural stay rather than for visiting a wide range of sites. Co. Waterford boasts a southern border of more than 50 miles/80km of coastland which is characterized by extensive bays, secluded beaches and cliffs, while inland the farm and hilly woodland is broken up by the Comeragh, Monavullagh and Knockmealdown mountains. This is excellent walking and cycling country, along with the Ballyhoura and Galty Mountain ranges of Tipperary, and the Mullaghareirk peaks of Limerick.

The area is well served by railways: the diagonal line from Limerick to Waterford via Clonmel couples with another from Cork to Portlaoise via Thurles to form a huge cross through the region, its diagonals meeting near Tipperary town. There are airports at Waterford and Shannon, just northwest of Limerick city, while trunk roads connect all the main centres. Buses connect Dublin with most main towns and with each other.

## Waterford Crystal Glass Factory

Kilbarry, Co. Waterford; ⓣ051/332500, ⓦwww.waterfordvisitor-centre.com; March–Oct, daily 8.30am–6pm; Nov–March Mon–Fri 9am–5pm, booking ahead advised, last tour Nov–Feb 3.15pm, March–Oct 4pm; adults €6, under 12s free, but no under 10s permitted in factory.

Children and adults alike are mesmerized by displays of skilled glass-blowing alongside the hot furnaces. Guided tours of this world-famous factory last an hour and include glass-cutting, engraving and sculpting and there is a film on the history of glass making in Ireland.

## Reginald's Tower

The Quay, Waterford city; ⓣ051/304220; Easter–May, Mon–Fri, 10am-5pm; June–September, Mon–Fri, 9.30am–6.30pm; October Mon–Fri, 10am–5pm; Open Weekends 10am–5pm; call for winter opening details; adults €2, children €1.

Originally built by the Vikings, there's been a Reginald's Tower on Waterford Quay for more than a thousand years, during which it has functioned as a fortress, a mint and a prison. It now holds a new exhibition about its own past and that of the Viking and medieval periods. Today's tower dates back to the 12th century, and has been completely restored to its medieval magnificence.

## Waterford Treasures

Merchant's Quay, Waterford city; ℡051/304500; ⓦwww.water-fordtreasures.com; daily April, May & Sept 9.30am–6pm, June–Aug 9.30am–9pm, Oct–March 10am–5pm; adults €4, children 5-16 €2, family €10.

A splendid museum detailing the city's history from Viking times onwards through seven audiovisual presentations (including a 3-D audiovisual sea voyage) and interactive displays and plenty of interesting artefacts including Viking and Anglo-Norman jewellery and weaponry mostly dug up in the last twenty years.

## Cahir Castle

Cahir, Co. Tipperary; ℡052/41011; ⓦ www.heritageireland.ie; daily, mid-March to mid-June & mid-Sept to mid-Oct 9.30am–5.30pm; mid-June to mid-Sept 9am–7.30pm; mid-Oct to mid-March 9.30am–4.30pm; adults €2.75, children €1.25, family €7. Heritage Card.

A magnificent, well-preserved castle situated on a rocky island on the River Suir that variously dates from the thirteenth to the nineteenth centuries. It has all the extras children expect, such as a keep complete with portcullis and vaulted chambers, a moat, dark, spooky walks, a prison accessed by a trap door, plenty of turrets and musket loops. There is a short video on the locality and a coffee shop.

## Mitchelstown Cave

Burncourt, Cahir, Co. Tipperary; ℡052/67246; ⓦwww.mitchel-stowncave.com; daily, 10am–6pm; adults €3, children €1.

The guided tour of these impressively damp and echoing, caves take you half a mile through three large caverns with stalactites, stalagmites, calcite crystals and a 30ft-high calcite column.

## Ormond Castle

Carrick-on-Suir, Co. Tipperary; ℡051/640787; mid-June to Sept daily 9.30am–6.30pm for guided tours; adults €2.75, children €1.25, family €7. Heritage Card.

A beautiful Elizabethan mansion tacked onto the remains of a fourteenth-century castle complete with two towers built in the mid-fifteenth century.

## Brú Boru, Cultural Centre

Cashel, Co. Tipperary; ☎062/61122; ⓦwww.comhaltas.com;
June–Aug, Tues–Sat, 9am–11.30pm, Sun & Mon 10am–5pm,
Sept–May, Mon–Fri 9am-5pm; exhibition: adults €5, children €3,
entry to centre free.

Buried in chambers seven metres below the Rock of Cashel,
the Sounds of History exhibition (a bit heavy-going for the
under-10s, to be honest) examines Ireland's traditional music
from ancient times onwards. There are performances of traditional Irish music from mid-June to mid-September, Tues–Sat
at 9pm, which your younger ones might enjoy.

## Cashel Folk Village

☎062/62525; daily 10am–7.30pm; adults €2.50, children €1.
Located in the lane behind the tourist office, this museum
has items relating to Republican history as well as a gory
reconstruction of a butcher's shop, a pub, a forge, and so on.

## Rock of Cashel

Co. Tipperary; ☎062/61437; ⓦwww.heritageireland.ie; daily mid-
March to mid-June 9am–5.30pm, mid-June to mid-Sept
9am–7.30pm, mid-Sept to mid-March 9am–4.30pm; adults €5,
children €2, family €11. Heritage Card.

One of the top six visitor attractions in Ireland, a staggering
sight from a distance and equally enthralling when you get
there, the Rock of Cashel is a huge limestone outcrop upon
which rises a collection of medieval Christian buildings
including a cathedral, church, round tower and castle tower
house. In contrast with these majestic sites, a mile out on the
road to Clonmel is the tiny Bothan Scoir (☎062/61360; visits by prior arrangement), a miserable seventeenth-century
one-roomed peasant dwelling.

## Parson's Green Leisure Park

Co. Tipperary; ☎052/65290; ⓦ www.clogheen.com; mid-March
to Sept 10am–8pm; adults €3, children €2, family €10.

By the Knockmealdown Mountains, this riverside attraction
features farm and pet animals including sheep, goats, emus
and llamas, an agricultural museum, woodland walks, crazy
golf, boat trips, pony rides, playgrounds and a coffee shop.

## Museum of Transport

Richmond Mill, Clonmel, Co. Tipperary; ☎052/29727; Mon-Sat
10am-6pm; adults €3, children €2.

Displays at this small museum include vehicles going back to
the 1930s, such as Rolls Royces, Fords, Jaguars as well as
motorbikes, petrol pumps, roadsigns and other motoring
memorabilia.

## Folk Farm and Transport Museum

Fethard, Co. Tipperary; ℡052/31516; Sun noon–6pm and by appointment; €2.50.

At the start of the Cashel road, this museum housed in a former railway station has twelve hundred exhibits including hearses, horse-drawn carriages, penny farthings and other bicycles, Victorian prams and everyday household items from a century ago.

## Nenagh Heritage Centre

Nenagh, Co. Tipperary; ℡067 33850; Apr–Oct, Mon–Fri, 10am–4pm.

Once North Tipperary's county gaol, and later a school, today it is home to models of Lough Derg and two lakeside villages – Dromineer and Garrykennedy. Fascinating though these miniature worlds are, expect the family to come away ruminating on the condemmed cells, the gloom of the prison, and the pithy biographies of some of those whose lives ended here.

## Croom Mills

Croom, Co. Limerick; ℡061/397130; ⓦwww.croommills.ie; daily 9am–5pm; free.

The large cast-iron water-wheel of this corn-grinding mill is powered by the River Maigue. There is a century-old steam engine, alongside interactive exhibits and a video about the history of Croom Mills and the milling process.

## Foynes Flying-Boat Museum

Co. Limerick; ℡069/65416; ⓦwww.webforge.net/foynes/; April–Oct daily 10am–4pm; adults €4.40, children €2.20.

This museum celebrates late 1930s and early 1940s Foynes when the town was a staging post for the transatlantic flying boat service. Children will enjoy the radio and weather room, where original transmitters, receivers and Morse Code equipment are on show.

## King John's Castle

Nicholas Street, Limerick town; ℡061/360788; ⓦ www.shannon-heritage.com; daily mid-April–Oct 9.30am–5.30pm, Nov–mid-April 10.30am–4.30pm; adults €7, children €4.20, family €17.50.

One of Ireland's best Anglo-Norman castles, despite the modern entrance spoiling the huge gateway. Kids will love dragging their parents up to the battlements for panoramic views of the city. There are displays of medieval weaponry, a twenty-minute film of the history of the city and an interpretive centre focusing on the Normans in Ireland.

# Sport and activities

## Bicycle rental

**Emerald Cycles**, 1 Patrick Street Limerick, ⓉⒸ061/416983; **Murphy Cycles**, Main Street, Dungarvan, Co. Waterford ⓉⒸ058/41376.

## Boat cruises

**Galley River Cruises**, Waterford, ⓉⒸ051/421723. Lunch (€20, two hours), dinner (€38, three hours) and evening tea (€10, two hours) river trips to New Ross from June to August, children 1/3rd off.

## Horseriding and pony trekking

**Homeleigh Farmhouse**, Ballinacourty, Glen of Aherlow, Tipperary Town, ⓉⒸ062/56228; **Tipperary Mountain Trekking Centre**, Rusheen, Borrisoleigh, Nenagh, Co. Tipperary, ⓉⒸ0504/51055; **Hillcrest Equestrian Centre**, Hillcrest House, Gallbally, Co. Limerick, ⓉⒸ062/37915.

## Swimming

**Civic Swimming Pool**, Borstal Square, Clonmel Co. Tipperary, ⓉⒸ052/21972; **Splashworld**, Tramore, Co. Waterford, ⓉⒸ051/390176, Ⓦwww.splashworld.ie.

## Water and adventure sports

**Dunmore East Adventure Centre**, Dunmore East Harbour, Co. Waterford, ⓉⒸ051/383783, Ⓦwww.dunmoreadventure.com; Summer camps for 10-17 year-olds and various adventure sports including windsurfing, sailing, canoeing, climbing and archery.

# Accommodation

**Cashel Holiday Hostel**, 6 John Street, Cashel, Co. Tipperary, ⓉⒸ062/62330, Ⓦwwww.cashelhostel.com; A good, centrally located hostel, from €13 per person, including children.
**Clonea Strand Hotel**, Clonea, Dungarvan, Co. Waterford, ⓉⒸ058/45555, Ⓦwww.clonea.com; The hotel complex has a holiday cottage for seven (€295–895 per week plus a leisure centre with swimming pools, tennis, tenpin bowling and playgrounds.
**Homeleigh Farmhouse**, Tipperary, ⓉⒸ062/56228. Four miles south of Tipperary, a B&B that also offers pony trekking and fishing.

**Kilmaneen Farmhouse**, Clonmel, Co. Tipperary; ☏052/36231, ⓦwww.kilmaneen.com; Open Easter–Sept. Kilmaneen offers comfortable B&B accommodation (€37.50 per person) on a remote working dairy farm with good walks and two-bedroom self-catering cottage €350–500 per week.

**McEniss Ard Rí Hotel**, Ferrybank, Waterford; ☏051/832111, ⓦwww.jurysdoyle.com; Overlooking both the city and the River Suir, although this chain hotel is rather bland, there are extensive grounds, a leisure centre with pools, a gym for rainy days, babysitting and a kid's room in July and August.

**Park House Farmhouse**, Stradbally, Co. Waterford; ☏051/293185. Ideal for secluded sandy Stradbally Cove. Rooms cost from €26.50 per person per night.

# Places to eat

**Haricot's Wholefood Restaurant**, 11 O'Connell Street, Waterford City; ☏051/841299. Cosy good value cafe with staples like pasta, vegetable soup, lentil casserole from €8.50, half portions €5.

**Mr Bumbles**, Kickham Street, Clonmel, Co. Tipperary; ☏052/29188. Informal eaterie with anything from coffee and cakes to full steak suppers.

**The Parrish**, 41-42 Mary Street, Dungarvan, Co. Waterford; ☏058/45700. Inexpensive but good snacks and meals including sandwiches, soups, potato wedges, panini, from €3–5.

**The Tannery**, 10 Quay Street Dungarvan, Co. Waterford; ☏058/45420. Modern menu that, though not cheap, is very good value for money. Children welcome until 8.30pm.

# 8

# Cork

Cork is Ireland's largest county and one of the most popular with families visiting the country. As well as the lively and charming port city of Cork, there's beautiful mountain scenery, peaceful lakes, and a coastline of spectacular cliffs, quiet beaches and coves to enjoy.

Although the railway will only really take you off to visit other counties to the north, the roads are at their best in the south of Co. Cork, and buses reach everywhere important.

## Blarney Castle

☎021/438 5252, ⓦwww.blarneycastle.ie; May & Sept, Mon–Sat 9am–6.30pm, Sun 9.30am–5.30pm; June–Aug, Mon–Sat 9am–7pm, Sun 9.30am–5.30pm; Oct–April Mon–Sat 9am–6pm/sunset, Sun 9.30am–sunset; €7.

Just a few miles northwest of Cork, this castle, built in 1446, is notable for housing the famous Blarney Stone, which even quite young visitors will queue up for, so that they can be dangled over. Legend suggests that a kiss of the stone will give you gift of the gab, and its fame has caused the town to grow into something of a tourist centre. You may have to wait an hour for your chance at the stone during the summer months. Be warned, it's sited some 80ft above the ground; you'll need a head for heights to reach it.

## Cork city centre

Cork city is built on an island, and is ideal for wandering around, to take in the sights and atmosphere. The centre is sandwiched between two channels of the River Lee and there are plenty of cafés, restaurants and interesting shops to look at, as well as Crawford Municipal Art Gallery (Emmet Place/Paul Street, Mon–Sat 10am–5pm; free) with its impressive collection of Irish art. The English Market off Princes Street is worth a detour on your wandering, for the food stalls and the delicious products on sale.

## Cork Gaol

Convent Avenue, Sunday's Well, Cork City, Co Cork; ☎021/430 5022, ⓦwww.corkcitygaol.com; daily March–Oct 9.30am–6pm, Nov–Feb 10am–5pm, last admission one hour before closing; adults €5, children €3, family €14.

Suitable for all ages, the atmosphere of this former prison is re-created using life-size wax figures and eerie sound effects. The exhibition looks in depth both at heroes of the early republican era – who stayed here before being transported to Australia – and at stories of the ordinary men, women and children locked up from the pre-Famine era to the foundation of the Irish state, often for crimes that would now seem quite trivial, in conditions of unimaginable cruelty.

## Cork Heritage Park

Blackrock, Cork city, Co Cork; ☎021/435 8854; Easter–Sept around noon–5pm daily but opening times can vary; adults €3, children €1.50.

As well as the many animals to be seen in the pet farm, aviary and duck pond, there is an activity centre where children can draw and paint, with exhibitions on the Cork Fire Service and the city's maritime history.

## St Anne's Shandon

Shandon Street, Cork city; ☎021/450 5906; daily May–Sept 10am–6pm, Oct–April 10am–5pm; €5 per person.

This prominent church sits nearby the old butter market at the top of a hill overlooking the River Lee. Children will love it not only for its weather vane, an eleven-foot gold fish, but for its tower, which can be climbed for a great view and a ring of the bells.

## Dursey Island cable car

Mon–Sat 9–11am, 2.30–5pm & 7–8pm and variable Sun.

On a windy day kids and parents will be wailing with excitement and delight as they take the six-minute cable-car ride across the slim sound from the furthest tip of the Beara Peninsula to Dursey Island. It's perfectly safe, of course, but the views make it an unforgettable experience. Even though there's nothing to do on the island but enjoy the bracing walks and look at the houses, it will be a memorable day. The cable car has room for just three passengers and a cow, so you may have to go in two groups, and you'll find it at the end of the R572 road.

## Fota Wildlife Park and Fota House

Fota Island, Carrigtohill, Co Cork; ☎21/481 2678, ⓦww.fotaw-ildlife.ie/; mid-March–Oct Mon–Sat 10am–6pm, Sun 11am–6pm, last admission 5pm, Nov–mid-March Sat 10am–4pm, Sun 11am–4pm, last admission 3pm; adults €7, children 3-16, under 2s free, family €27.90.

This park, ten miles from Cork city (off the N25 road or Fota's own station on the Cork city-Cobh line), has more than ninety species in open surroundings, with those not in cages left free to roam. There are playgrounds, a tour train, gift shop and self-service cafe, as well as the Fota Arboretum and Gardens adjacent. Fota House (ⓦwww.fotahouse.com; April–Sept Mon–Sat 10am–5.30pm, Sun 11am–5.30pm, Oct–March 11am–4pm; adults €5, children €2, family €12), which sits in the middle of the grounds, is of limited interest to most children. It's a smart, early nineteenth-century hunting lodge. Rooms on show include the dining room, the hall and its gallery, and the servants' quarters.

## Queenstown Story

Cobh Heritage Centre, Railway Station, Cobh; Ⓣ021/481 3591, ⓦwww.cobhheritage.com; Nov–Feb 10am–5pm, March–Oct 10am–6pm; adult €5, child €2.50, family €15.50.

Few children's ears don't prick up at the mention of *the Titanic* which stopped at Cobh on its tragic maiden voyage, one of the subjects covered at this multimedia attraction. *The Lusitania*, her sister ship, also stopped off here on her final voyage, which again, ended in tragedy. *Lusitania* was torpedoed and sank with equally massive loss of life (many victims were buried at Cobh). This action led directly to the US joining the first World War. The port was also a departure point for those destined for the Napoleonic wars, for emigrants heading to America and for convicts transported to Australia in the nineteenth century. Further insight into Cobh's dramatic past can be found at the Cobh Museum (Easter–Oct, Mon–Sat 11am–1pm & 2–6pm, Sun 3–6pm; €1.50).

## Charles Fort

Summer Cove, Kinsale, Co Cork; Ⓣ021/477 2263, ⓦwww.her-itageireland.ie; mid-March–Oct 10am–6pm, Nov–mid-March Sat & Sun 10am–5pm; adult €3.50, children €1.25, family €8.25.

Built between 1678 and 1682, this star-shaped fortress was involved in one of Ireland's most important historical events, the Williamite War (1689–92). The main attraction as far as the kids are concerned will be the interactive exhibits, which let them have a go at designing a fort of their own, using the touch-screen displays.

## Schull Planetarium,

Schull; Ⓣ 028/28315 or 28552, ⓦhomepage.tinet.ie/~planetari-um/. Christmas holidays, Easter weekend, bank holidays and May–Sept: phone for details. Adults €4.50, children € 3.20, family ticket (2 adults & 2 children) €12.00. Shows last for 45mins. and are unsuitable for children under 7.

Perched next to the harbour, this is the only planetarium in the country, built by the enthusiastic amateur stargazer, Josef Menke. The late Herr Menke enjoyed many holidays in Cork with his family and built the planetarium in this tiny fishing village as a permanent "thank you". It opened in 1989 and, since then, The Starshow has been a great success, and a must-see attraction. All shows are presented by live and experienced lecturers, who welcome questions from children and adults alike in the sessions immediately afterwards.

## Skibbereen Heritage Centre

Upper Bridge Street, Skibbereen, Co. Cork; ℡028/40900, Ⓦ www.skibbheritage.com; mid-March–mid-May & mid-Sept–Oct, Tues–Sat, 10am–6pm; mid-May–mid-Sept, daily, 10am–6pm; adult €4, child €2, family €9.

Located in the beautifully restored old gasworks building, the heritage centre contains exhibitions, dramatizations and interactive exhibits on the Great Famine, which greatly affected the town (there are mass graves at Abbeystrewery nearby, where almost 10,000 are buried). There is also an interpretive centre explaining the unique marine life of nearby Lough Hyne, a landlocked salt lake, with a saltwater aquarium containing species from the lake

## Fox's Lane Folk Museum

Fox's Lane, Youghal, Co Cork; ℡024/91145; July & Aug Tues–Sat, 10am–1pm & 2–6pm; open by appointment rest of year; adults €4, children €2, family €10.

This museum, tucked away in the centre of a holiday resort town, is home to more than 600 domestic appliances and gadgets that have outlived their time. Dating from around 1850 to 1950, the exhibits include gramophones, old-style telephones, cast-iron sewing machines, immensely heavy typewriters, vacuum cleaners, and more unusual items such as cucumber straighteners, a wasp trap and petrol-fuelled clothes irons. Children find all this ancient quirky history fascinating and a visit here will entertain the parents too.

## Perks Family Entertainment Centre

Seafield Business Centre, Youghal, Co Cork; ℡024/92438, Ⓦ www.perksfunfair.com; free admission, prices for activities vary

Kids can really let their hair down here. There are funfair rides (including a ghost train and crazy mirrors), snooker, pool, ten-pin bowling, video games, an ice-cream parlour and fast-food restaurant to entertain them for hours.

# Sport and activities

## Bike rental

**An Stór Hostel**, Drury's Avenue, Midleton, ☎021/463 3106; **CycleScene**, 396 Blarney Street, Cork, ☎021/430 1183; **The Hire Shop**, 18 Main Street, Kinsale ☎021/477 4884; **MTM Cycles**, 33 Ashe Street, Clonakilty ☎023/33584; **Rothar Cycles**, 55 Barrack Street, Cork ☎021/431 3133; **N. W. Roycroft and Son**, Ilen Street, Skibbereen ☎02821235.

## Boat rental and cruises

**Atlantic Boating Service**, Baltimore; ☎028/22734, Ⓦwww.atlanticboat.ie; You can rent a motor-boat here that will seat six or so for €250 per week or €65 per day.
**Harbour Queen Ferries**, Glengarriff; ☎027/63116. Ten-minute trips past basking seals to Garinish Island cost €10 for adults, and €5 children. If you want to visit the island too, there's an additional charge (adults €3.50, children €1.25).
**Marine Transport Services**, Atlantic Quay, Cobh; ☎021/481 1485). Harbour boat trips, June–Sept, adults €5, children €3.
**Naomh Ciarán Ferries**, Baltimore; ☎028/39135. Ferry trips to Clear Island, taking 45min, adults €11.50 return, children €6.

## Horseriding

**Bantry Horse Riding**, Bantry; ☎027/51412. Classes and treks for children as well as adults.

## Swimming

**Gus Healy Swimming Pool**, Douglas Road, Cork, (☎021/429 3073); **Leisureworld**, Rossa Avenue, Bishopstown Cork; ☎021/434 6505).

## Watersports and adventure sports

**Atlantic Sea Kayaking**, Union Hall; ☎028/33002, Ⓦ www.atlanticseakayaking.com. River and sea kayaking trips and courses.
**International Sailing Centre**, Cobh; ☎021/481 1237, Ⓦwww.sailcork.com. Sailing, power-boating (over 12s only) and canoeing courses.
**Oysterhaven Activity Centre**, Kinsale; ☎021/477 0738, Ⓦ www.oysterhaven.com. Sailing, wind-surfing, canoeing, kayaking and equipment/boat rentals.
**Trabolgan Holiday Village**, MidletonⓌ021/466 1551. All-weather entertainment including archery, abseiling, badminton, basketball, crazy golf and swimming. Closed Nov-March.
**West Cork Sailing Centre**, AdrigoleⓌ027/60132. Kayaking, powerboating, sailing.

# Accommodation

**An Stór Hostel**, Drury's Avenue, Midleton; ☎021/463 3106.
Dorms, twins and family rooms in a converted mill. €14.50 per
person for family rooms.

**Barley Cove Holiday Park**, Crookhaven; ☎028/35302; Easter
and May–mid-Sept. Accommodation is in self-catering mobile
homes at €365 per week in July and August for a six-berth.
Convenient for a great beach, the park also has tennis courts, a
café/takeaway and bicycles for rent.

**Bay View,** Old Timoleague Road Clonakilty; ☎023/33539,
ⓦwww.bayviewclonakilty.com; closed Nov–Feb. Immaculate,
bright B&B at €28-35 per person with a 33% reduction for kids.

**Jurys Cork Inn**, Anderson Quay, Cork; ☎021/427 6444,
ⓦwww.jurysdoyle.com; Accommodation of a high standard that
is especially good value for families. Rooms (€80–89) can
accommodate two adults and two children under 12.

**Westlodge Hotel**, Bantry; ☎027/50360, ⓦwww.westlodgehotel
Upmarket modern hotel (family room for two adults and two children, €140) with pool, gym, tennis and squash, self-catering cottages (from €500 for two-bed sleeping four) and organised family
activities June–Aug.

# Places to eat

**Kalbo's Bistro**, 48 North Street, Skibbereen; ☎028/21515.
Informal, offering good-value lunches such as baguettes and
baked potato from about €8.

**Pak Fook**, Youghal; ☎024/90668. Chinese food, always a winner
with children.

**Pizza Republic**, 97 South Main Street, Cork; ☎021/427 9969.
Laid-back bistro with moderately-priced wide choice including
kid's pizza and pasta dishes for €6.

**Quay Co-op**, 24 Sullivan's Quay, Cork; ☎021/431 7026.
Vegetarian/vegan self-service cafe for breakfast, lunch, tea, dinner and children's portions.

**Spanish Point Restaurant**, Ballycotton; ☎ 021/464 6177. Well
appointed overlooking Ballycotton Bay, children can get half portions of the €23 lunches, such as chicken and chips and pasta
dishes.

# 9

# Kerry

It is not difficult to fathom why Kerry is eternally popular with visitors: it contains some of Ireland's best scenery, made up of rugged coastline, mountain, moorland and lakes, coupled with a great choice of accommodation and places to eat. True, sections of the county get overrun by tourism at times,

## Information

Tourist offices are at Dingle, ☎066/915 1188; Kenmare,
☎064/41233 (April–Oct); Killarney, ☎064/31633; Listowel,
☎068/22590 (June–Sept); and Tralee, ☎066/712 1288.

especially around the 110-mile Ring of Kerry, Ireland's most
popular scenic route. Yet the crowds and tourist kitsch are
always easy to escape, and it is an ideal place to enjoy a great
variety of family entertainment, from swimming and beach-
combing to cycling, boating and water sports.

Roads and therefore bus routes fan out in all directions
from the two main towns, Tralee and Killarney, and a railway
line stretches from Tralee to Killarney and the east.

## Crag Cave

Castleisland; ☎066/714 2144, ⓦwww.cragcave.com; mid-
March–June & Sept–Oct daily, 10am–6pm; July & Aug, daily
10am–6.30pm; adults €6.50, children €4, family €20.

This well-lit network of limestone caves was only discovered
in 1983 yet is more than a million years old. It extends two
miles underground and the thirty-minute guided tour passes
numerous stalactites and stalagmites. There is an indoor play
area for children aged under 9 (extra charge) as well as craft
shop and café.

## Coolwood Park

Coolwood, Coolcaslagh, Killarney, Co. Kerry; ☎064/36288;
June–Sept 11am–6pm, weather permitting; adults €4, children
€3, family €17.

This wildlife park and sanctuary has all kinds of birds and
beasts, some of which children can take part in feeding. There
are also nature walks, a coffee shop and a playground with
slides, swings and aclimbing frames.

## Oceanworld

Dingle; ☎066/915 2111; ⓦwww.dingle-oceanworld.ie; May &
Sept, daily 10am–6pm; June, daily 10am–7pm; July & Aug, daily
10am–8.30pm; Oct–April, Mon–Sat, 9am–4.45pm, Sun
10am–4.45pm; adults €8, children €5, family €22.

This centre for marine conservation on the waterfront is not
massive, but still has around thirty tanks including a touch pool,
a tropical coral reef display in the shark tank and a tunnel tank
to walk through. There is a new turtle exhibition and children
can help feed the fish and staff walk around the aquarium with
some creatures, such as lobsters and crabs, so that they can be
seen up close. After seeing more than a hundred species of fish
and other marine life, holding a starfish and stroking a ray, you
can take a walk along the beautiful Dingle Peninsula.

## The Freshwater Experience

Emlagh, Lispole, Co. Kerry; ⓣ066/915 1042; March–Oct,
Mon–Sat, 9.30am–6pm, Sun noon–6pm.

As well as having a wildlife park with otters, wild boars,
mink, foxes and other animals, there is a reserve that is home
to a number of species of goose, duck and swan. There are
ancient Celtic monuments and a medieval lake dwelling.

## Kennedy's All-weather Pet Farm and Playground

Glenflesk, Killarney, Co. Kerry; ⓣ064/54054;
ⓦwww.kennedys.rural-biznet.com; April–Oct, 10am–7pm;
Nov–March, 10am–5pm; €6 per person

Five miles from Killarney town centre on the N22 Cork
road, this working dairy and sheep farm also has puppies, kit-
tens, rabbits, pigs, goats, ducks, geese, donkeys, and many
more birds and animals. Many can be handled and fed by visitors. There are free pony rides, indoor and outdoor playgrounds and traditional farm machinery on display.

## Killarney Model Railway

Beech Road, Killarney, Co. Kerry; mid-March to Oct & Dec daily
10.30am–6pm; adults €4, children €2, family €10.

More than a mile of track and more than 55 operating trains
makes this one of the world's biggest model railways. Many
landmarks of Europe are depicted, as well as Killarney town
itself, and there is an enchanting night-time display. Children
can also test their skills on the centre's model car racing track.

## Killarney National Park

Killarney, Co. Kerry; visitor centre: mid-March–June, Sept & Oct
daily, 9am–6pm; July & Aug, daily 9am–7pm; free

About a third of this beautiful park is made up three lakes
and almost parallel to its western border is a glacial breach
called the Gap of Dunloe. There is a visitor centre at
Knockreer House with a twenty-minute audiovisual about
the park, along with other information. Bicycles can be hired
in Killarney, and there are various tours by a combination of
boat, pony trap, bus and bike, and guided walks on foot.
Enquire at Killarney tourist office.

## Muckross Estate

Muckross, Killarney, Co. Kerry; ⓣ064/31440, ⓦwww.muckross-
house.ie; house: daily, 9.30am–5.30pm; farms: mid-March–April
& Oct, Sat & Sun 1–6pm; May, daily 1–6pm; June–Sept, daily
10am–7pm; joint ticket for house and farms: adult €8.25, children €3.75, family €21; friary: mid-June–early Sept daily
10am–5pm; free; gardens: open all year; free.

The various attractions of Muckross Estate combined can make for a pleasing, if not ecstatic, day for the family. Muckross House is a nineteenth-century neo-Elizabethan mansion, livened up somewhat for visitors by its installation of craftspeople demonstrating such things as weaving, bookbinding and pottery. There is also the ruin of a Norman and Gothic friary, extensive gardens, walks to Muckross Lake, a good café-restaurant in the crafts centre and three traditional working farms where actors reconstruct day-to-day farming life in years gone by and such activities as potato picking, harvesting and hay-making can be seen, depending upon time of year. Children can also experience a trip on a vintage coach.

## Museum of Irish Transport

East Avenue Road, Killarney, Co. Kerry; ☎064/34677; daily, March–Oct 10am–6pm, Nov–Feb 11am–4pm; adults €5, children €2, family €12.

This excellent museum has plenty of well-preserved vintage cars including the world's rarest car, the Silver Stream, built in 1907, of which only one was manufactured. There are also fire engines, carriages, bicycles and motorbikes, as well as a 1930s workshop.

## Fenit Sea World

The Pier, Fenit, Tralee, Co. Kerry; ☎066/713 6544; daily Easter–Oct 11am–5.30pm; adults €5.50, children €3.50, family €17.50.

Aquarium with marine life from Tralee Bay and the Atlantic Ocean. Kids might be more interested in the timbers of a haunted shipwreck, a submarine labyrinth and a re-creation of the gloomy ocean floor can also be seen.

## Kerry the Kingdom at Kerry County Museum

Ashe Memorial Hall, Denny St, Tralee, Co. Kerry; ☎066/712 7777, Ⓦ www.kerrycountymuseum.com; mid-March–Oct daily 10am–6pm; Nov–Dec 24, 11.30am–4.30pm; adults €8, children €5

Accounts of the history of Ireland and Kerry from the first settlers in 8000BC to the declaration of the Irish Republic in 1948. Audiovisual presentations, reconstructions and archaeological treasures as well as temporary exhibitions are livened up by the Irish Medieval experience, where visitors take a "time-car" ride past a re-creation of streets and buildings of fifteenth-century Tralee.

## Scanlon's Pet Farm

Ballydavid, Tralee, Co. Kerry; ☎066/915 5135; mid-April–Sept, Mon–Fri 10am–6pm, Sun 2–6pm; adults €3, children €1.50, family €10.

Surrounded by countryside and overlooked by Mount Brandon, this farm has animals that include deer, geese, pigs, peacocks and rabbits, many of which be fed by children in the mornings. There are indoor and outdoor playgrounds, river walks and a picnic area.

## Tralee to Blennerville Steam Railway and Blennerville Windmill

☎066/712 1064 or ☎066/712 8899; train: April–Sept, Tues–Sun hourly, but check first; return adult €5, child €2.50; windmill: April–Oct daily 10am-6pm; adult €4, child €2
You can still travel this section of the Tralee-Dingle line, which ran from 1891 to 1953, a fifteen-minute journey, at the end of which is Blennerville Windmill, Ireland's biggest working windmill. There's the usual exhibition on the locality, with audio-visuals and craft workshops, but it's the windmill itself that's the real attraction.

# Sport and activities

## Bicycle rental

**Altazamuth**, Valentia Island, ☎066/947 6300; **Casey's**, Main Street, Cahersiveen, ☎066/947 2474; **Glenross Caravan and Camping Park**, Glenbeigh, ☎066/976 8451, ⓦwww.killarney-camping.com (May–mid-Sept); **O'Sullivan's Cycles and Outdoor Store**, Bishop's Lane, New Street, Killarney, ☎064/31282; **Trailways Outdoors Centre**, College Street, Killarney, ☎064/39929, ⓦwww.trailwayskillarney.com; **Tralee Gas Supplies**, Strand Street, Tralee, ☎066/712 2018.

## Boat trips and ferries

**Blasket Ferries**, Ventry; ☎066/915 6422. Boats to Great Blasket Easter-Oct, €20 return.
**Flannery's**, Dingle; ☎066/915 1967. Offers two-hour boat trips (€15, wetsuit hire €20) enabling participants to swim with Fungi, Dingle harbour's resident dolphin.
**Seafari**, Kenmare; ☎064/83171; ⓦwww.seafariireland.com; Five cruises from the pier July/Aug, with the possibility of spotting whales, seals and dolphins. Children get to enjoy a puppet show, sweets and face painting too.
**Skellig Heritage Centre**, Portmagee; ☎066/947 6306, ⓦwww.skelligexperience.com; Cruises around Skellig Michael Island (1hr 45min; €21) and Knightstown and around the harbour (60min; €17), the price includes the exhibition on the locality at the heritage centre.

**Valentia Island Ferry**, Reenard Point; ℡066/947 6141. Every 15 minutes to 10pm April–Sept. Cars return €7, cyclists return €3, pedestrians €2.

## Fishing

**Trailways Outdoors Centre**, College St., Killarney; ℡064/39929; ⓦwww.trailwayskillarney.com; Fishing trips and boat hire.

## Horseriding

**Killarney Riding Stables**, Killorglin Road, Ballydowney, Killarney; ℡064/31686, ⓦwww.killarney-reeks-trail.com; Horseriding in the county's national park for adults and children aged over eight. One hour is €25 per person.
**Long's**, Ventry; ℡087/225 0286. From €20 per hour for mountain and beach riding, minimum age 8.

## Quad bikes

**Waterville Quad Safari and War Game Adventures**; ℡066/947 4465, ⓦwww.actionadventurecentre.com; Two-hour quad tours for older drivers (€60) and Kiddie Quads for 6–14 year-olds and a purpose-built track (€25). There is also a combat game for those aged 10 and over (€55).

## Swimming

**Aqua Dome**,Tralee; ℡066/712 8899, ⓦwww.discoverkerry.com/aquadome; April–Aug: adults €9, children €8, Sept–March: adults €8, children €7. Huge water slides, wave and whirl pools, rapids and water cannons, and next door 18-hole miniature golf course, Aqua Golf.

## Watersports and adventure sports

**Cappanalea Outdoor Education Centre**, Killorglin; ℡066/976 9244. Canoeing, wind-surfing, rock-climbing and other outdoor activities.
**Jamie Knox Watersports**, Castlegregory; ℡066/713 9411, ⓦwww.jamieknox.com; Activities like surfbiking, paddle-boating and snorkelling. Canoeing, for example, €6 per hourp; five-session windsufing course for under 12s, €120.

# Accommodation

**Gleneagle Hotel**, Kenmare Road, Killarney; ℡064/36000, ⓦwww.gleneagle-hotel.com; The good leisure facilities, pool and restaurants make this a good family choice. One night in high season, family room with two adults, two children €300.

**Glenross Caravan and Camping Park**, Glenbeig; ℗066/976 8451, Ⓦwww.killarneycamping.com; May to mid-Sept. Lots of facilities including shop, laundries, TV and games rooms, forest and riverside walks; Caravan and tent per night €6 plus €5.50 adult, €1.50 child under 14.

**Killarney International Hostel**, Aghadoe Road, Killarney; ℗064/31240. Three miles northwest of the centre and ideal for the mountains, there are family rooms (€50 winter, €80 summer, two adults and two children per night), bike rental and a free bus to and from the bus and train stations.

# Places to eat

**The Bricin**, 26 High Street, Killarney; ℗064/34902. Cosy restaurant with traditional Irish food on the menu like boxties (potato pancakes). Adult meals €14-20 and set two courses €21 with half-portions for kids. Also children's menu, €6.

**Broadbery's**, The Square, Killorglin; ℗066/976 2888. Café-restaurant and attached deli with good seafood and vegetarian dishes and child portions.

**The Moorings**, Portmagee; ℗066/947 7108, Ⓦwww.moorings.ie; Restaurant and bar, averaging €35 for three-course meal with children's menu (chicken nuggets and chips etc) €5.

**Out of the Blue**, Strand Street, Dingle; ℗066/915 0811. Seafood deli and restaurant with outside tables and child-sized portions.

**QC's**, 3 Main Street, Cahersiveen; ℗066/947 2244; winter Thurs–Sun only. Very accommodating, by asking what children like to eat, also children's menu with chicken nuggets/fishfingers and chips €6.50. Adult meals €12.

# 10

# Clare

With some of Ireland's most stunning landscapes, County Clare can provide a visitor with a wide range of experiences, from the musical traditions kept very much alive in energetic Ennis, the lively county town, to the bleak tranquility of the Burren, a seemingly endless expanse of limestone and shale.

The coast is scattered with wonderful sandy beaches and little seaside villages and there are plenty of opportunities for water sports. The county has plenty of gentle farmland, which is ideal for cycling. The many small lakes north of Dysert O'Dea are ideal for fishing.

A spiders' web of roads spread out from Ennis, in the centre of the county, and there is a once- or twice-daily train from Ennis to Limerick (one hour) and to Dublin (three hours). Buses serve most areas daily, and run at least hourly during the day to and from Bunratty, Ennis and Limerick to Shannon Airport.

### Aillwee Cave

Ballyvaughan,,Co. Clare; ℡065/707 7036; ⓦwww.ailweecave.ie; daily 10am–6pm; adults €e8, children €4.50, family €22.

The surprise underground world of this fascinating limestone cave formed in a prehistoric ice age in the Burren is revealed in the 30min tours over bridged chasms, caverns of stalagmites and stalactites, a frozen waterfall, curious rock formations and hibernation chambers of extinct brown bears. A thundering waterfall occasionally sprays visitors and children will enjoy looking out for the calcite formations in the form of such things as praying hands and a wasp's nest. Back outside the cave children can stretch their legs on a nature trail through woodland. As well as a gift shop and tearoom, cheese can sometimes be seen being made in the dairy or honey being extracted from combs.

### Newtown Castle

Ballyvaughan,,Co. Clare; ℡065/707 7200; May–Sept 10am–4pm; free.

This sixteenth-century fortified tower has all the features that children find interesting – battlements, narrow slit windows, gun loops and murder holes, while the nature trail adjacent to the castle takes you on a mile-long trip around the Burren.

### Bunratty Castle and Folk Park

℡061/360788, ⓦwww.shannonheritage.com; June–Aug daily 9am–6pm, Sept–May daily 9.30am–5.30pm combined ticket for castle and folk park: adults €10, children €5.60, family €26.25.

A strategically important site since Viking times (AD 970),

the existing castle is Ireland's most complete medieval castle. Built in 1460 it boasts a well-restored keep. Bloodthirsty fledgling knights can discover the dungeon and inspect the castle's "murder holes" where attackers would be met with a barrage of boiling water or oil. The folk park, although perhaps over-touristy, brings history to life for little ones by re-creating a nineteenth-century village complete with a water-mill, church, ten farmhouses, a schoolhouse, doctor's house, merchant buildings and shops. There is a forge, printing press and bakery, and costumed characters bring the "village" to life.

## Riches of Clare Exhibition

Clare Museum, Arthur's Row, Ennis, Co. Clare; ☎065/682 3382; ⓦwww.clarelibrary.ie; Jan & Feb, Oct–Dec Mon–Fri 9.30am–1pm & 2–5.30pm, March–May Mon–Sat 9.30am–1pm & 2–5.30pm, June–Sept daily 9.30am–5.30pm; adults €3.50, children 5–12 €1.50, family €10.

This sleek, permanent exhibition in the county's modern museum makes intelligent use of interactive displays, inform-ative commentary and lively audiovisual presentations to throw light on to the past. Packed with intriguing items that range from an ancient human hipbone pierced by a prehis-toric arrow to examples of more modern weaponry used by the IRA, and including Clare's connection to the Spanish Armada, the museum also has a traditional hearth scene where the children can sit and listen to an old Clare folk tale. A good day's worth of entertainment all in one building.

## Knappogue Castle

Near Quin, Ennis, Co. Clare; ☎ 061/360788; ⓦ www.shannon-heritage.com; April-Oct daily 9.30am-5.30pm; adults €4, children €2.30.

A wonderfully restored fifteenth-century castle that puts on its own medieval banquets (April–Oct twice nightly 5.30pm–8.45pm, subject to demand). There is also a newly-restored nineteenth-century walled garden and formal garden for your little lords and ladies to let off steam.

## The Burren Centre

Kilfenora, Co. Clare; ☎065/708 8030; ⓦwww.theburrencentre.ie; mid-March–May, Sept & Oct 10am–5pm, June–Aug 9.30am–6pm. €3.

A combination of models of castles and forts, and touch-screen and audiovisual displays including an effective 3-D map of the Burren region and a film tracing its evolution, and explanations of the natural history, plant and animal life, geology and archaeology of this famously harsh region.

# Lahinch Seaworld

Lahinch, Co. Clare; ☎065/708 1900,
Ⓦwww.lahinchseaworld.com; daily, opening times vary; swimming, sauna and Jacuzzi: adults € 7, children 5-16 €5, children 2–4 €3; aquarium only adults € 7, children 5-16 €5, children 2–4 €3, combined swimming and aquarium tickets adults € 12, children 5–16 €8, children 2–4 €4; playzone: under 12s €4.

Lahinch effortlessly provides a complete family day out with its aquarium featuring a ray pool, wave tank, touch pools, lobster breeding station, ocean tank and more, while kids can play at being fish themselves in the 25-metre swimming pool and kiddies pool. Finally, there's a playzone for the under 12s featuring crawl tubes, a tube slide, ball pools and pendulum swings.

# Moher Hill Open Farm & Leisure Park and Cliffs of Moher

Cliffs of Moher Road, Liscannor, Co. Clare; ☎065/7081071;
Ⓦwww.moherfarm.com; Easter–Nov 10am–6pm; adults €5, children €4.

As well as the many inmates here including sheep, deer, llamas, goats, donkeys and ponies, a good day out is guaranteed at the indoor and outdoor play areas, which feature go-karts, sand diggers, mini-golf and a bouncy castle. Close by Liscannor, the Cliffs of Moher stretch for five miles, and are Clare's most majestic natural attraction. Accessible by well-marked footpath, they should not be missed.

# West Clare Railway

Moyasta Junction, Kilrush, Co. Clare; ☎065/905 1284;
Ⓦwww.westclarerailway.com; Mon–Sat 10am–6pm, Sun noon–6pm; €6 adults, €3 children.

A section of this 112-year-old narrow gauge railway line operates for tourist trips through the Clare countryside. Passengers get to ride in carriages built in the style of that period, pulled by a diesel locomotive. As well as the four-mile trip, visitors see the refurbished railway station and 1950s film of the train operating.

# The Craggaunowen Project

Kilmurry, near Quin, Co. Clare; ☎061/360788; Ⓦwww.shannon-heritage.com/Craggaunowen_Day.htm; mid-April–mid-Oct 10am–6pm; adults €7, children €4.20, family €17.50.

Craggaunowen explains how the Celts arrived and lived in Ireland. There are replicas of an Iron Age road, a fourth century ring fort, a hunter's cooking site and a Crannog, a Bronze Age lake dwelling made from wattles, reeds and mud. Craggaunowen Castle, built in 1550, stands on a crag overlooking the lake, and a replica of the "Brendan Boat", built

## Dolphin Watching

There are few better ways for children to appreciate the beauty and charm of these wonderful creatures than by meeting them close up, but from the safety of a boat. There are numerous companies offering dolphin-watching excursions, but these are among the best.

**Dolphinwatch**, The Pier, Carrigaholt; ℡065/905 8156, Ⓦwww.dolphinwatch.ie. Run daily two-hour trips from April to October, to see the resident group of bottlenose dolphins. Very child-friendly, there's even a toy box on board. Adults €18, children 2–16 €9.

**Dolphin Discovery**, Kilrush, Co. Clare; ℡065/905 1327, Ⓦwww.discoverdolphins.ie. This firm has a boat purpose-built for watching the Shannon Estuary bottlenose dolphins, equipped with a hydrophone so you can listen to them as well. Tours run April–Oct; adults €16, children €8.

and sailed from Ireland to Greenland by Tim Severin to echo the voyage of St Brendan, who was reputed to have discovered America long before Columbus.

# Sport and activities

### Bicycle rental

**Gleesons**, Henry Street Kilrush, ℡065/905 1127;,**Williams'**, Circular Road, Kilkee, ℡065/905 6041.

### Boat cruises and rental

**Derg Princess**, Killaloe Heritage Centre, The Canal, Killaloe; ℡065/376866. Hour-long cruises of Lough Derg May–Sept daily noon & 2.30pm; €7.
**Lakeside Watersport Caravan and Camping Park,** Mountshannon; ℡061/927225. Canoe (€3 per hour), sailboat (€22 per day) and motor boat (€40 per day) rental May–Oct.
**Whelan's Boat Hire**, Main Street, Killaloe; ℡061/376159. Boats for four with outboard engines.

### Horseriding and pony trekking

**Burren Riding Centre** Fanore; ℡065/707 6140. Riders aged eight and over, €20 per hour.
**Clare Equestrian Centre**, Deerpark, Doora, Ennis; ℡065/ 684 0136, Ⓦ www.clareequestrian.com; Treks starting from €20 per child, classes and pony camps.

**Clonara Equestrian Centre**, Oakfield, Clonara; ☎061/354172. Indoor and outdoor arenas, lessons, trekking and cross-country.

## Swimming

**Waterworld**, Circular Road, Kilkee; ☎065/905 6855. Kid-friendly pool with 200ft tower slide. Mon–Fri, midday–7pm; Sat–Sun 2–8pm. Closed end October–Easter.

## Traditional Irish Music

**Glór Irish Music Centre**, Friar's Walk, Ennis; ☎065/684 3103, ⓦwww.glor.ie. A national centre for the performance of Irish music with regular performances, some specifically aimed at children. Film, theatre, dance, visual arts and children's workshops also.

## Watersports and adventure sports

**Killaloe Activity Centre**, Killaloe; ☎061/376622. Hires out windsurfs, wetsuits, dinghies and canoes.
**Kilkee Diving and Watersports Centre**, Kilkee; ☎065/905 6707. Scuba-diving, prices vary.
**Kilrush Creek Lodge and Adventure Centre**, Cappa Road, Kilrush; ☎065/905 2855, ⓦwww.kcac.nav.to. Kayaking, canoeing, wind-surfing, powerboating, archery, raft-building, orienteering and sailing. Typically €15 per hour, €50 per day per activity.

# Accommodation

**Nagle's Camping and Caravan Park**, Doolin, Co. Clare; ☎065 7074458; May–Sept. Tremendous location between the Burren and the Cliffs of Moher
**West County Hotel**, Clare Road, Ennis; ☎065/682 3000, ⓦwww.lynchotels.com; A modern hotel less than a mile south of the centre with three swimming pools and a children's play centre. Rooms can accommodate two adults and two children and start at €79 per room.

# Places to eat

**Bofey Quinn's**, Main Street, Corofin; ☎65/683 7321. Family-friendly restaurant with wide selection of dishes including children's menu from €6.
**Ruby Tuesday's**, Merchants Square, Ennis; ☎065/684 0474. Good-value restaurant with family-friendly feasts such as pastas,

chicken nuggets/burger and chips, around €10 adults, €3.95 children.

**Strand Restaurant**, Kilkee; ℡065/905 6177, Ⓦwww.clareguest-house.com; On the seafront with good seafood and meat dishes (€16–25 adult) and a small selection of dishes for kids (€5.50).

**Whitethorn Restaurant**, Whitethorn Visitor Centre, Ballyvaughan; ℡065/707 7044; mid-March–Oct. Good food in a great setting, with children's portions.

# 11

# Galway, Mayo and Roscommon

Galway is a popular holiday destination for many visitors: the lively, culturally rich city of Galway, with its modern beach resort Salthill, is a convenient base for the splendid scenery of west Galway, notably the untouched wilderness of Connemara and its seemingly endless bog, heather-clad moorland and mountain. Children love the adventure of taking a ferry across to the stark Aran Islands, Inishmore, Inishmaan and Inisheer, with their sandy beaches. Roscommon and Mayo, in contrast, are so often overlooked as a holiday destination yet offer restful rural delights. Mayo is renowned by anglers, and boasts four great lakes as well as one of Ireland's most popular resort towns, Westport.

The region is well served by public transport. From Athlone a railway line stretches to Galway, with another reaching Westport via Roscommon and Claremorris, with a further line branching from Claremorris to Ballina. Roads and therefore buses reach most extremes of the three counties, with Galway being the greatest travel hub by far.

## Information

Tourist offices are, open all year unless otherwise stated, at Galway, ☏091/537700; Tuam, ☏093/25486 (mid-June to mid-Sept); Inishmore, ☏099/61263; Oughterard, ☏091/552808; Roundstone, ☏095/35815 (summer); Clifden, ☏095/21163 (March–Oct); Inishbofin, ☏095/45861/45895 (summer); Westport, ☏098/25711; Cashel, ☏098/47353; Killala, ☏096/32166; July–Sept; Vallina, ☏096/70848; Foxford, ☏094/925 6488; Cong, ☏092/46542 (March–Oct); and Roscommon, ☏0903/26342.

## Atlantaquaria

Toft Park, Salthill, Galway, Co. Galway; ☏091/585100, ⓦwww.atlantaquaria.com; Mon–Fri 10am–5pm, Sat & Sun 10am–7pm; adult €7, child €4, family €21.
This excellent aquarium includes a miniature version of Galway's waterways complete with docks, locks and salmon piers, and displays of native Irish aquatic life, with both seawater and freshwater fish. A child's perspective is always present, for example in the story of an Atlantic salmon's adventures en route for Greenland and back again.

## Dan O'Hara's Homestead and the Connemara Heritage and History Centre

Lettershea, Clifden, Co. Galway; ☏095/21246, ⓦwww.connemaraheritage.com; April–Oct daily 10am–6pm; adults €6, children €3.
This centre features a restored cottage and homestead, and reconstructions of a ring fort and lakeside dwelling all viewable by guided tour by tractor-bus. There are turf-cutting

demonstrations, sheep-herding and other activities demon-
strated for groups on request, as well as a twenty-minute
video on the history of the region, archaeological displays, a
craft shop and tea room.

## Connemara National Park

ⓣ095/41054; visitor centre: mid-March–May, Sept & Oct
10am–5.30pm, June 10am-6.30pm, July & Aug 9.30am–6.30pm;
adults €2.75, children €1.25.
Situated in the heart of the west of County Galway, this
beautiful area covers 2000 hectares of mountains, bog, heath
and grassland. The visitor centre on the west side of
Letterfrack village introduces the history, geology, wildlife
and plantlife of the park and is the starting-point of several
nature trails. An eighteen-minute audiovisual presentation
traces the natural history of Connemara and during July and
August there are organized childrens' days with art, fun and
games with nature as the theme.

## Ocean's Alive Sealife Centre

Connemara, Co. Galway; ⓣ095/43473; daily March–Sept
10am–7pm; aquarium and museum: adults €5, children €2.50;
aquarium, museum and cruise: adults €15, children €10.
Principally a maritime museum, this also has a small aquarium with fish of the locality such as starfish and rockpool
dwellers. Shipwrecks, boats and maritime artefacts such as
lobster pots and model boats explain local maritime history,
and you can take an hour-long wildlife cruise to nearby
uninhabited islands.

## Athenry Castle

Athenry, Co. Galway; ⓣ091/844797; ⓦwww.heritageireland.ie;
April, May & mid-Sept–Oct, Tues–Sun 10am–5pm; June–mid-
Sept daily 10am–6pm; adults €2.75, children €1.25, family €7.
Athenry's Norman town walls give the town a fortified,
mediaeval feel that kids will love, and the thirteenth-century
castle boasts a fantastic three-storey keep. A further Athenry
distraction is the heritage centre (daily 10am-6pm;
ⓣ091/844661, ⓦhomepage.tinet.ie/~athenryheritage/her-
itagecentre/heritage.htm; €3.50), situated in the eighteenth-
century church of St Mary's, with audiovisual displays of the
castle's history. Children can dress up in medieval costume,
try archery or get lost in the maze.

## Dartfield Horse Museum

Dartfield, Killreekill, Loughrea, Co. Galway; ⓣ91/843968;
ⓦwww.dartfieldhorsemuseum.com; daily 9am–6pm; €5.
Showing the use of the horse through history, this isolated

museum, surrounded by fields and paddocks, contains displays demonstrating the importance of the horse in the areas of transport, farming, sport and local traditions. Children can use the bank of computers to glean further equine information, and there is a rather tame riding machine, small play area, café and shop with riding gear and souvenirs.

## Glengowla Mine

Oughterard, Co. Galway; ☏091/552360; March–Nov daily 9.30am–6.30pm; adults €6.50, children €3.50.

Lively guided tours of the mine evoke the tough lives miners endured working by candlelight in this lead and silver mine worked between 1850 and 1865. They were often knee-deep in water, blasting the rock and drilling by hand. You can see many of the workings of the mine, including original ladders, pulley systems and pipes. On the surface is a blacksmith's workshop and cottage.

## Tumble Jungle

Ballina, Co. Mayo; ☏096/76637, ⓦwww.tumblejungle.ie; €5 per child per hour, 1–12 years.

This is Ireland's largest indoor play centre and features a huge space with five bouncy castles, a climbing frame with a two-storey obstacle course, a soft play area for toddlers and café.

## Maghu's Castle

Kiltimagh, Co. Mayo; ☏094/9374886; July–Aug, Mon–Fri noon–6pm; all year: Sat noon–6pm, Sun 2–6pm and at selected other times; €5 per child per hour 1–11 years, under 4ft 9in.

This brand new all-weather playground has everything the desperate parent could need on a rainy day: an adventure maze, rope bridge, slide, ball pond, aerial runway, punch bags and toddlers play area.

## Westport House

Westport, Co. Mayo; ☏098/27766, ⓦ www.westporthouse.ie; Easter–Sept, times vary; adults €15, children €10, family €49.

The main attraction for children of this grand stately home built in 1730 is the mini-railway, giant water slide and bouncy castle in the grounds. If that isn't enough, there are pedaloes, train rides, pitch and putt, rowing boats and an indoor play area. Add the dungeons (complete with spooky sound effects) and bird and animal park, and you've got a full, fun day out for all the family.

## King House

Main Street, Boyle, Co. Roscommon; ☏071/966 3242, ⓦwww.roscommoncoco.ie/kinghouse; daily April–Sept 10am–6pm; adults €4, children €2.50, family €10.

What could be a boring old restored Georgian mansion is brought to life using lifesize models and special effects within re-created scenes to trace the history of the elegant house. Children are encouraged to participate, whether dressing as a Gaelic chieftain or building a brick vault. Afterwards they can tackle the on-site adventure playground.

# Sport and activities

## Bicycle rental

**John Mannion**, Bridge Street, Clifden, ☎095/21160; **Sean Sammon**, James Street, Westport, ☎098/25471; **Mill House**, American Street, Belmullet, ☎097/81181; **Cong Hostel**, Headford Road, Cong, ☎092/46089.

## Boat cruises

**Corrib Princess**, Woodquay, Galway; ☎091/592447. Ninety-minute cruises daily from Woodquay.

**Killary Cruises**, near Leenane; ☎freephone 1800 415151, ⓦwww.killarycruises.com; This offers ninety-minute catamaran all-weather trips down Killary fjord.

**Island Ferries**, Victoria Place, Galway; ☎091/568093; ⓦwww.aranislandferries.com; Trips from Rossaveel to Inishmore (2–4 daily, 35min), Inisheer (1–2 daily, 60min) and Inishmaan (1–2 daily, 50min). Singles are €10, returns €19 with coach connections to and from Galway.

**Portumna Passenger Boat Company**, Portumna; ☎086/391 8364. Hour-long cruises of Lough Derg (June–Aug) and trips to Terryglass on the Tipparary side of the water (April, May, early Sept).

**Truelight**, Roundstone; ☎095/21034, ⓦwww.truelight.ie; Three-hour harbour cruises in a traditional hooker, €40.

## Horseriding and pony-trekking

**Carrowholly Stables and Trekking Centre**, Carrowholly, Westport, Co. Mayo, ☎098/27044, ⓦwww.carrowholly-stables.com); **Cleggan Trekking Centre**, Clifden, ☎095/44746; **Drummindoo Equitation Centre**, Westport, ☎098/25616; **Mulrany Riding School**, Newport, ☎098/36126; **Errislannan Manor**, Clifden, ☎095/21134; **Laragan Stables**, Clifden, ☎095/44735; **Renvyle House**, Renvyle, Co. Galway, ☎095/43511, ⓦwww.renvyle.com.

## Leisure centre

**Mayo Leisure Point**, Moneen, Castlebar, Co. Mayo; ℡94/25473, Ⓦwww.mayoleisurepoint.ie. Ireland's largest indoor entertainment park with a cinema, rollerball, karting, video games and bowling.

## Swimming

**Leisureland**, Salthill, Galway; ℡091/521455; daily year round, opening hours vary; adult €7, children €4.80. This leisure complex in Salthill has a swimming pool with slides, a kiddie's pool, pirate ship and crazy golf. Nearby in Salthill is Perk's funfair, mega trampolines, remote controlled boats and bungee jumping.
**Westport Leisure Park**, Westport; ℡098/29160. This place features a swimming pool with a kid's obstacle course.

## Watersports and adventure sports

**Atlantic Adventure Centre**, Louisburgh Road, Westport; ℡098/64806. Sailing courses for all.
**Hodson Bay Watersports**; ℡1890 704090, Ⓦwww.hodsonbay.com; Tour Lough Ree by powerboat.
**Little Killary Adventure Centre**, Leenane; ℡095/43411, Ⓦwww.killary.com; Day and residential courses from rock-climbing to mountain biking, sail-boarding, archery, kayaking and wind-surfing.
**Scuba Dive West**, Glasilaun Beach; ℡095/43922, Ⓦwww.scubadivewest.com; Courses and diving off the coast.
**Surf Mayo**, Westport; ℡087/621 2508. Surfing instruction, wetsuit and surfboard hire.

# Accommodation

**Ardilaun House Hotel**, Taylor's Hill, Galway; ℡091/521433, Ⓦwww.ardilaunhousehotel.ie; Kids can stretch their legs in the five acres of woodland around this hotel and there's a swimming pool for rainy days.
**Glen Valley House**, Glencroff; ℡095/42269. A working farmhouse where kids can meet the resident Connemara ponies.
**Jurys Galway Inn**, Quay Street, Galway; ℡091/566444, Ⓦwww.jurysdoyle.com; The spacious comfortable rooms here are at a flat room rate and sleep up to four, and are therefore ideal for families on a budget.
**Marless House**, Threadneedle Road, Galway; ℡091/523931, Ⓦww.marlesshouse.com; Cosy and on the coast, children especially welcome here and there are special family deals.
**Renvyle House**, Renvyle, Co. Galway; ℡095/43511, Ⓦwww.ren-

vyle.com; An upmarket hotel where kids will love the swimming pool, tennis, boating and horseriding.

# Places to eat

**Ard Bia**, 15 Cross Street, Galway; ℗087/236 8648, ⓦwww.ard-bia.com; A great little café and coffee shop in the funky part of town with good vegetarian selections.

**Dolphin Restaurant**, Inishbofin; ℗095/45992. Seafood, meat and vegetarian options.

**Quay Cottage**, Westport; ℗098/26412. Seafood and vegetarian restaurant.

**Two Dog Café**, Church Hill, Clifden; ⓦwww.twodogcafe.ie; Good coffee, great food – sandwiches, tortilla wraps, salads – and internet access.

# 12

# Sligo and Leitrim

These two counties both have luscious scenery. Sligo is known for the beautiful mountains Benbulben and Knocknarea and including the major parts of the gorgeous Glencar and Gill loughs, as well as some marvellous beaches to the west at Enniscrone and Strandhill and to the north at Streedagh Strand. The rolling farmland of south Sligo is renowned for its traditional music. Sligo town itself is a lively, bustling, traffic-clogged place which might have plenty of amenities, but isn't the best place for families to stay.

In terms of population, Leitrim is the smallest county in Ireland, home to a mere 26,000 people. Often neglected by tourists, its northern mountains and glens and its many lakes, including the vast Lough Allen, remain largely unexploited. With its riverside setting, Carrick-on-Shannon is a popular boating centre, as well as being the county's largest town.

## The Cavan and Leitrim Railway

Dromod, Co. Leitrim; ☎071/963 8599, Ⓦhomepage.eircom.net/%7Eyarpie/clr/. April–Sept Mon–Fri 10am–5pm, Sun 1–5.30pm; train rides €5 per person.

Operating from a restored station on the old Cavan and Leitrim Railway, right next to the existing Dublin–Sligo main line, enthusiasts run regular trips, in fantastic old trains pulled by unusual engines, half a mile up the narrow gauge track to Clooncolry (although there are plans to continue onwards to Mohill). At the time of writing the CLR had acquired a number of old aircraft too and these may soon be on display in the station yard.

## Culkin's Emigration Museum

Dromore West, Co. Sligo; ☎096/914 7152. June–Sept Mon–Sat 11am–5pm, Sun 1–5pm; adults €3, children €2.

Daniel Culkin's Shipping and Emigration Agency operated on this spot from the nineteenth century to the 1930s and arranged for many Sligo people to leave for a better life in the USA. The museum contains the original Agency shop, depicts life in post-Famine Ireland and recounts the tales of some of those locals who emigrated, something to ponder in these days of a booming Irish economy.

## Waterpoint

Pier Rd, Enniscrone, Co. Sligo; ☎096/36999,
Ⓦwww.showround.com/waterpoint. July & Aug Mon–Fri
10am–10pm, Sat & Sun 10am–8pm; Sept–June Mon–Fri 4–10pm,
Sat 1–8pm, Sun 11–8pm; adults €7, children €4.50, infants €3.
This modern complex offers a heated swimming pool and a
children's special fun pool, as well as a massive 210-feet-long
water slide. There's also fitness, sauna, jacuzzi and steam room
facilities for adults and a snack bar.

## Coleman Heritage Centre

Gurteen, Co. Sligo; ☎071/918 2599, Ⓦwww.colemanirishcen-
tre.com; Mon–Sat 10am–5pm, also April–Sept Sun noon–6pm;
AV display adults €4, children €2.
Erected in honour of Ireland's most influential traditional fid-
dler, Michael Coleman (1891–1945), who hailed from nearby
Killavil, this offers an audiovisual display on his life together
with various interactive touchscreens supplying information
on traditional music. Best of all, however, are the evening
shows of traditional music and dance, usually by local musi-
cians (April–Oct Weds & Sat), a great alternative if you want
to hear some traditional sounds but don't want to take your
kids to the pub. The centre also stocks an excellent range of
CDs and books.

## Gillighan's World

Knocknashee, Lavagh, Co. Sligo; ☎071/913 0286,
Ⓦwww.gillighansworld.com; May–early Sept Tues–Sun
11am–7pm; adults €6, children €5.
Knocknashee literally means "hill of the fairies", a place
with long-standing associations with the little folk, and
Gillighan's World is an imaginative attempt to enlighten
and entertain visitors about fairy life and lore. Its elegant
mountainside setting combines botanical gardens and
miniature villages populated by natural flora and fauna.
There are ponds and a trout lake, too, plus a pet village and
play area and, in December, the place transforms itself into
"Winter Wonderland".

## Irish Raptor Research Centre, Ballymote

Portinch, Ballymote, Co. Sligo; ☎071/918 9310, Ⓦwww.eagles-
flying.com; May–Nov daily 10.30am–12.30pm & 2.30–4.30pm;
adults €6, children €4, family €18.
Ireland's largest sanctuary for birds of prey and various breeds
of owl offers displays daily at 11am and 3pm, where various
falcons, vultures and eagles can be observed free-flying, while
younger children will enjoy the small pet zoo, featuring various farm animals plus rabbits and guinea pigs.

## Sligo Folk Park

Millview House, Riverstown, Co. Sligo; ⓉO71/916 5001, Ⓦwww.sligofolkpark.com; May–Oct daily 10am–4.30pm; adults €5, children €3, family €14.

Aiming to offer an insight into rural life at the end of the nineteenth century, the park's re-created village street features a forge, creamery, pub and grocery, and occasional craft demonstrations, while the museum includes many other artefacts and memorabilia. The park occupies the grounds of the restored Millview House and offers a nature trail along the banks of the Unshin river.

## Sligo Abbey

Abbey St, Sligo town, Co. Sligo; ⓉO71/964 6406, Ⓦwww.heritageireland.ie; Mid-March to Oct daily 10am–6pm; Nov & Dec Fri–Sun 9.30am–4.30pm; adults €2, children €1, family €5.50.

Though everyone calls it an abbey and it's on Abbey Street, these pretty, well-preserved ruins are actually those of a mid-thirteenth-century Dominican friary which served as such until the building was sacked during the rebellion of 1641. As the town's only surviving medieval building, it's well worth visiting for its many carvings, including Gothic and Renaissance tomb sculptures, elegant cloisters and fifteenth-century high altar. Tours are available on request and provide an informed insight into the life of the friars.

## Carrowmore Megalithic Cemetery

Sligo town, Co. Sligo; ⓉO71/916 1534, Ⓦwww.heritageireland.ie; Easter–Oct daily 10am–6pm; adults €2, children €1, family €5.50; Heritage card.

The biggest cemetery of Megalithic tombs in Ireland lies some three miles from Sligo town centre off the R292 Strandhill road. So far, some sixty tombs have been located in this field and scientific analysis suggests that some may date as far back as 5400BC, all good for bringing to life ancient man and his exploits. There's a restored cottage here which houses a small, but very informative, account of the site. High on a hill above is the sixty-foot high Medb's Cairn (known locally as "Maeve's Lump"), reputed to be the grave of the legendary Queen Medb of Connaught.

## Parke's Castle

Fivemile Bourne, Co. Leitrim; ⓉO71/916 4149, Ⓦwww.heritageireland.ie; Mid-March to Oct daily 10am–6pm; adults €2.75, children €1.25, family €7; Heritage card.

This restored seventeenth-century Plantation castle is a real gem of a building, positioned in a romantic setting on the shore of Lough Gill. The Parke in its name was one Robert who employed the walls of a previous moated castle to build his own home. The previous owner, the chieftain Brian O'Rourke, was hung for high treason at Tyburn in London in 1591 for sheltering a Spaniard from the wrecked Armada. Much of the castle's structure is still in very good shape and its rooms inside, including the forge, have been tastefully restored using traditional crafts and Irish oak. Next to the castle is a sweathouse. Boat trips around the lough leave from the landing stage here daily in summer.

## Glencar Waterfall

Glencar Forest, Co. Leitrim; open access.

Situated some seven miles west of Manorhamilton, Glencar Lough is a secluded spot and something of an angler's paradise thanks to its stocks of salmon and trout. From the car park by the lough's northern shore, a pathway rises upwards to this stunning waterfall, some fifty feet high and, obviously, best seen after heavy rainfall.

## Swan Island Open Farm

Keeldrin, Corrawallen, Co. Leitrim; ℡049/433 3065, ⓦhome-page.tinet.ie/~sweetjoni/swanisland/index.html. May–Oct daily 11am–6pm; call for prices

Swan Island is beautifully situated on the shore of Garadice Lake. The farm features more than fifty species of traditional and rare breeds and such delights as a ride in a pony cart. There's a children's play area and the two-hundred-year-old Davy's Cottage, which houses a restaurant (open from 6pm). The farm also opens in December for visits from Santa. To get here, take the R199 Killeshandra road from Ballinamore to Newtowngore then follow the Swan Island signs.

# Sports and activities

## Adventure centres

**Lough Allen Adventure Centre**, Ballinagleragh, Co. Leitrim; ℡071/964 3292.

## Boat rental and cruises

**Ballinamore Boats**, 3 Railway Rd, Ballinamore, Co. Leitrim; ℡071/964 4079. The Sliabh an Iarainn Sunset (Ireland's first wheelchair accessible waterbus) runs daily sailings on the Shannon-Erne waterways (June–Sept daily, Oct–May Sat & Sun) and evening trips to Swan Island Open Farm for dinner and music at Davy's Cottage. Rental also available.

**The Innisfree Tour Boat**, Kilmore, Five Mile Bourne, Co. Leitrim; ⓣ071/916 4266. Operates daily sailings around Lough Gill (March–Oct) picking up passengers at Riverside in Sligo town and Parke's Castle.

**Moon River**, Main St, Carrick-on-Shannon, Co. Leitrim; ⓣ071/962 1777, ⓦwww.moon-river.net. Runs 90-minute week-day afternoon trips along the Shannon during high season with extra sailings at weekends.

**The Blue Lagoon**, Riverside, Sligo town, Co. Sligo; ⓣ071/914 2530. Rental

## Cinemas

**Gaiety Cinema**, Bridge St, Carrick-on-Shannon, Co. Leitrim, ⓣ071/962 1869; **Gaiety Multiplex**, Wine St, Sligo town, Co. Sligo, ⓣ071/917 4002.

## Fishing

Several boats offer fishing trips from Mullaghmore and cruises to the deserted island of Innishmurray, including: **Excalibur Innishmurray Tours**, ⓣ087/245 0190; **Lomax Boats and Angling**, ⓣ071/916 6124; **Peter Power**, ⓣ087/257 6268 and, **Gerry Sheerin**, ⓣ071/916 6472. Prices depend on the length of the trip and the number of people sailing.

## Horseracing

**Sligo Race Course**, Cleveragh Rd, Sligo town; ⓣ081/918 3485, ⓦwww.air.ie/sligo.html. Meetings during 2004 on April 25, June 29, July 11, August 5 and August 18; adults €6–10, children under-14 free.

## Horseriding

**Co. Sligo**: Ard Chuan Equestrian Centre, Corbala, ⓣ096/45084; Island View Riding Stables, Island View, Grange, ⓣ071/916 6156, ⓦwww.islandviewridingstables.com; Markree Castle Riding Stables, Markree Castle, Collooney, ⓣ071/913 0727, ⓦwww.markreeridingstables.ie; Sligo Riding School, Carrowmore, ⓣ071/916 1353; Woodlands Equestrian Centre, Loughill, Lavagh, Tubbercurry, ⓣ071/918 4220.

**Co. Leitrim**: Drumcoura City, Ballinasloe, ⓣ071/964 5708; Hayden Equestrian Centre, Bornacoola, Dromod, ⓣ071/963 8049; Moorlands Equestrian Centre, Curraghill, Drumshanbo, ⓣ071/964 1500.

## Surfing schools

**Perfect Day Surf School**, Strandhill, Co. Sligo, ⓣ071/916 8464; **Seventh Wave Surf School**, Easky, Co. Sligo, ⓣ096/49020.

Otherwise visit the **Surf and Information Centre** in the centre of Easky; July & Aug daily 9.30am–5pm, Sept–June Mon–Fri 10am–2pm; ℡096/49020.

## Swimming

**Carrick Swimming Pool**, Carrick-on-Shannon, Co. Leitrim, ℡071/962 1400; **Sligo Sports Complex**, Cleveragh, Sligo town, Co. Sligo, ℡071/916 0539.

# Accommodation

**Beach Hotel and Leisure Club**, The Harbour, Mullaghmore, Co. Sligo; ℡071/916 6103, Ⓦwww.beachhotelmullaghmore.com. Overlooking the Atlantic, the Beach has its own swimming pool and gym and is ideally set for plenty of outdoor activities. It offers a babysitting service and a range of special breaks, from as low as €42.50 per person with child reductions.

**Dunfore Farmhouse**, Ballinfull, Lissadell, Co. Sligo; ℡071/916 3137. Set near the beach with views of Benbulben and Sligo Bay, this spacious farmhouse B&B offers four rooms suitable for families from €30 per person with child reductions, a putting green and lawn croquet; open March–Oct.

**Gortmór House**, Lismakeegan, Carrick-on-Shannon, Co. Leitrim; ℡071/962 1439. A farmhouse B&B, a mile or so northeast of Carrick, with a family room and its own Shetland ponies; from €26.50 per person with child reductions.

**Millhouse**, Keenaghan, Ballymote, Co. Sligo; ℡0918/3449, Ⓦwww.sligo-accommodation.com. Superb B&B in a tranquil South Sligo location with its own tennis court and award-winning breakfasts; from €25.50 per person with a third off for children.

**The Old Rectory**, Fenagh, Ballinamore, Co. Leitrim; ℡071/964 4089, Ⓦwww.theoldrectoryireland.com. A beautiful Georgian house in a delightful setting – very welcoming to families; from €32 for two people with 25 percent child reductions.

# Places to eat

**MJ Carr** and **The Loft Restaurant**, Lord Edward St, Sligo town, Co. Sligo; ℡071/914 6770. Downstairs is a railway-themed bar offering a daily carvery lunch while upstairs The Loft serves the most extensive menu in the county.

**Castle Arms Hotel**, Main St, Enniscrone, Co. Sligo; ℡096/36156. Excellent home cooking and carvery lunches.

**Cryan's**, Bridge St, Carrick-on-Shannon, Co. Leitrim. Fine bar serving substantial and highly popular meals.

**Eithna's Seafood Restaurant**, The Harbour, Mullaghmore; ☎071/916 6407. Local seafood, caught by one host and cooked by the other with organic meat and vegetarian options; open Easter–Nov daily 6.30–9.30pm.

# 13

# Donegal

With its bluff headlands and thrilling seascapes, multitude of loughs and staggering mountains, you could easily spend two weeks in Donegal and regret that you had not planned for a longer stay. The opportunities for outdoor activities are extensive and there are several seaside resorts (Bundoran

being the most popular), as well as plenty of places for families to visit on inclement days. However, without your own
transport getting around the county is not easy, especially out
of season.

### Ards Forest Park

Ⓣ 074/912 1139. April–Sept daily 10am–9pm; Oct–March, daily
10am–4.30pm; free.
Situated on the N56 between Creeslough and Dunfanaghy,
this twelve-hundred acre park provides plenty of scope for a
family outing. Its varied terrain comprises sandy beaches,
rivers and woodland and there are several way-marked nature
and walking trails plus picnic and play areas. The park is
home to a wide variety of bird life, as well as a herd of red
deer, and rarely gets crowded thanks to its car parking limit
of two hundred vehicles.

### Deane's Equestrian Centre and Open Farm

Darney, Bruckless; Ⓣ 074/973 7160, Ⓦ deanesequestrian@eir-
com.net. Open farm: April–Aug 10am–4pm; €4 per person.
Horseriding: all year.
This long-established open farm has a variety of animals and
birds on show and also offers pony rides (€3.50) and children's riding lessons (from €6 for fifteen minutes to €14 for
one hour), as well as trekking for more advanced riders (children must be aged 10 or over).

### Grianán Ailigh

Burt. Daily dawn–dusk; free.
Set a steep mile up a hill above Burt village, the Grianán
Ailigh dates back to around 1700BC and is a remarkable circular fort, prominent enough in the past to have been included in Ptolemy's second-century AD map of the world, and
the base for various northern Irish chieftains. However, by
the nineteenth century much of its stone had been carried
away and it was reconstructed by an archaeologist from
Derry in the 1870s. The views of Inishowen, the loughs and
other parts of the Donegal countryside from here are simply

## things not to miss

*You'll never manage to see everything the country
has to offer in a single trip – and we don't suggest
you try. But we've made a selection of activities
and attractions that we think represents the best
the country has to offer families, to help you get the
best out of your trip.*

**01** **Skellig Michael** Page **82** • One of Ireland's classic
seascapes – and most spectacular ferry destinations

**02 Open Farms** Page **147** • Making hay while the sun shines; open farms offer unforgettable days of peace and quiet

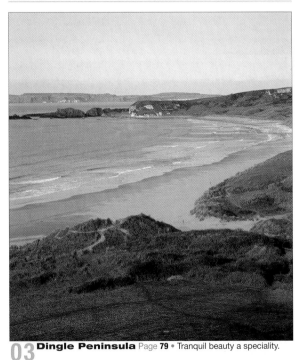

**03 Dingle Peninsula** Page **79** • Tranquil beauty a speciality.

**04** **Sailing** Page **104** • Ireland's a fantastic place to take your family afloat.

**05** **Fishing** Page **3** • Ireland's national sport

**06** **Pony trekking** Page **150** • Whether it's along the wild coast-line or through dreamy rural valleys, there's no better way to appreciate the country.

**07** **Galway City** Page **93** • A lovely old city that's full of surprises.

**08** **Grub! And plenty of it!** Page **6** • You'll not go hungry if these two have anything to do with it.

**09** **Dun Moher Castle** Page **88** • One of the most magnificent of Ireland's many prehistoric sites.

**10** **Fungi the dolphin** Page **80** • Famous for entertaining visitors to Dingle, he's a fun guy to be around

**11** **Hurling** Page **3** • Nothing matches the thrills of a hurling match.

**12 The Giant's Causeway** Page **127** • Arguably the world's oldest adventure playground.

**13 The Golden Ship** Page **15** • Don't miss the Viking treasures of the National Muaseum.

**14 Walking** Page **3** • "Come on now, will you? It's just over this next hill."

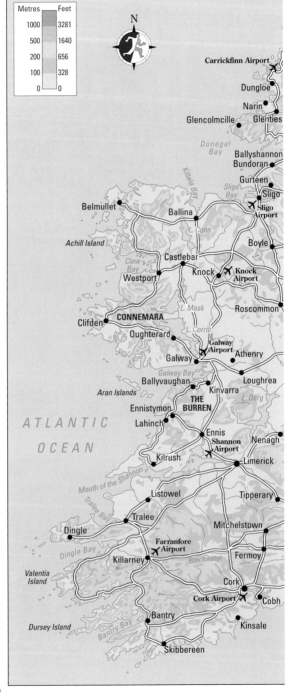

| Metres | Feet |
|---|---|
| 1000 | 3281 |
| 500 | 1640 |
| 200 | 656 |
| 100 | 328 |
| 0 | 0 |

N

Carrickfinn Airport ✈

Dungloe

Narin

Glencolmcille    Glenties

*Donegal Bay*

Ballyshannon
Bundoran

Gurteen

*Sligo Bay*    Sligo

✈ Sligo Airport

Belmullet    Ballina

*L. Conn*

*Achill Island*    Boyle

Castlebar

*Clew Bay*    Knock    ✈ Knock Airport

Westport

*L. Mask*    Roscommon

**CONNEMARA**

Clifden    Oughterard    *L. Corrib*

✈ Galway Airport

Galway    Athenry

*Galway Bay*    Loughrea

Ballyvaughan

*Aran Islands*    Kinvarra    *L. Derg*

**THE BURREN**

Ennistymon

Lahinch    Ennis
Shannon ✈ Airport

*ATLANTIC*    Nenagh

*OCEAN*    Limerick

Kilrush

*Mouth of the Shannon*    Tipperary

Listowel

*Tralee Bay*    Mitchelstown

Tralee

Dingle    Farranfore ✈ Airport    Fermoy

*Dingle Bay*    Killarney    *Blackwater*

*Valentia Island*

Cork

Cork Airport ✈    Cobh

Bantry    Kinsale

*Dursey Island*    *Bantry Bay*

Skibbereen

**15 Newgrange** Page **41** • One of the most important stone age sites in Europe.

**16 Traditional Music** Page **7** • A skilled player is guaranteed an appreciative audience, and company too.

**17 Kilmainham Gaol** Page **13** • Now restored and reopened as a visitor attraction.

**18 Carrick-a-rede rope bridge** Page **125** • Just keep telling yourself that it's perfectly safe, and try not to look down.

**19 A visit to the pub** Page **6** • A drink, a chat, a quiet sit down to watch the world pass by.

**20 Kissing the Blarney Stone** Page **72** • And for ever-more you'll have the gift of the gab.

**21 Boat trips** Page **2** • "Oh, a life on the ocean wave..."

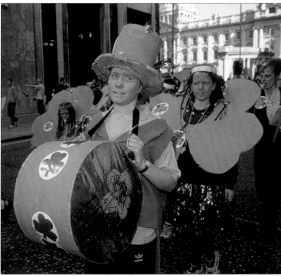

**22** **St Patrick's Day Parade, Belfast** Page **7** • The green face paint is optional, but having fun is not.

**23** **Connemara Countryside** Page **93** • The hills and valleys stretch out into the distance, without end.

**24** **The Burren** Page **86** • Unique, and outstandingly beautiful. The road goes ever on and on.

**25** **Viking Splash Tours** Page **21** • Take home memories of this very different way to see the sights of Dublin.

**26** **Horseracing** Page **3** • Ireland's other national sport.

**27** **Ulster Folk and Transport museum** Page **137** • One of the thirty or so typical buildings making up the "museum village".

**28** **Galway Arts Festival** Page **7** • Where even a man dressed as my little pony can have a great time.

**29** **Festivals and fairs** Page 7 • You can't beat getting up close and personal.

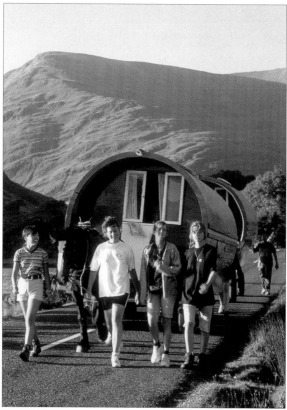

**30** **The open road** Page 1 • Take to the highways in a traditional gypsy caravan, and the whole country lies at your feet.

stunning. Back in Burt, the Grianán Ailigh Centre (daily: June & Aug 10am–7pm, Sept–May noon–4.30pm; ℡074/936 8000, Ⓦwww.griananailigh.ie; €5 per person) lays on an exhilarating audiovisual account of the fort's history and a return minibus trip to the fort (handy for those without transport).

## Millbridge Open Farm

Convoy; ℡074/914 7125. July & Aug, Tues–Sat 11am–5pm, Sun 1.30–5pm; adults €5, children €3.

There's all manner of farm animals here to meet and touch, plus wagon rides, an adventure play area and the opportunity to paddle a canoe or row a boat (activities cost an additional €1–1.75 per person).

## Doagh Visitor Centre

Doagh Island, Inishowen; ℡074/937 8078. Easter–Oct, daily 10am–5.30pm; €5 per person.

Through buildings such as a fairy house and a re-created farm cottage plus various tableaux, the centre provides a wealth of information on local customs while its Famine Walk offers a challenging account of the effects of the Great Hunger and draws parallels with the contemporary situation in Africa. From late November until Christmas it transforms itself into "Donegal's Lapland" complete with an Xmas show, reindeer, an elves kingdom and, of course, Santa (nightly 5pm; adults €7, children €14 including present from Santa).

## Donegal Bay Waterbus

The Quay, Donegal town; ℡074/972 3666, Ⓦwww.donegalbay-waterbus.com; Easter–Sept, daily, weather permitting – call for times; adults €10, children €5, family tickets available on request.

The Waterbus takes you on a ten-mile trip around Donegal Bay, lasting just over an hour, and passing such sites as the old Abbey, the burial place of the chieftain Red Hugh O'Donnell and the ruins of O'Boyle Castle. It also sails past oyster- and mussel-beds and offers the chance to view plenty of bird life and a colony of seals.

## Donegal Castle

Tirconnaill St; ℡01/074 972 2405, Ⓦwww.heritageireland.ie). Mid-March–October, daily 10am–6pm; Nov & Dec Fri–Sun 9.30am–4.30pm; adults €3.50, children €1.25, family €8.25; Heritage card.

Donegal Castle can trace its origins to a tower house constructed by the Gaelic chieftain Red Hugh O'Donnell in the fifteenth century, but was rebuilt and extended by Sir Basil Brooke who was given command of the town after the English defeat of the second Red Hugh in 1603. Various displays recount the castle's history, but the real enjoyment lies in taking a guided tour of its richly furnished rooms, some hung with French tapestries, and marvelling at the building's combination of strong defence and domestic splendour.

## Donegal Railway Heritage Centre

Old Station House, Tirconnaill St, Donegal town; ⓣ 074/972 2655, ⓦ www.countydonegalrailway.com; Year-round, Mon–Fri 10am–5pm; June–Sept, Sat & Sun 2–5pm; adults €3.50, children €2, family €8.

The Heritage Centre is devoted to recapturing the delights of the old narrow gauge Donegal County Railway (or "Wee Donegal" as it was affectionately known) which ran all the way from Derry to Ballyshannon, for one hundred years until 1959. The Centre has photo displays, models and railway artefacts, and a simulator lets you imagine driving a steam train through the Barnesmore Gap, it also has a working model railway and enthusiasts are busy restoring old rolling stock in the yard.

## The Workhouse

Dunfanaghy; ⓣ 074/913 6540. Mon–Fri 10am–5pm, Sat & Sun noon–5pm; adults €4, children €2.

Dunfanaghy's workhouse was built in 1845 just before the outbreak of the Great Famine. However, as the hunger took its toll, by 1847 it was housing over six hundred people. The story of one local inmate "Wee" Hannah Herrity is recounted upstairs through a series of tableaux each with its own commentary. Downstairs houses a coffee shop, an art gallery displaying temporary exhibitions and a craft and book shop.

### Beaches

Donegal's coastline includes a number of startlingly good beaches, many seeming to stretch for miles of golden sand. However, be advised that some are not suitable for swimming because of changing tides and strong undercurrents; and bring your own picnic as few of the most enjoyable ones are near catering facilities. Amongst the best are: Tullan Strand, Buncrana; Rossnowlagh; Murvagh (near Donegal town); Maghery (look out for the Assarancagh Waterfall on the way from Ardara); Narin (where you can walk out to Inniskeel Island at low tide); Magheraroarty; Falcarragh; and, on the Inishowen Peninsula, Tullagh Strand, Pollan Strand, Culdaff and Kinnego Bay.

# Fort Dunree Military Museum

Dunree, Inishowen; ☎ 074/936 1817, ⓦ www.dunree.pro.ie;
June–Sept, Mon–Sat 10.30am–6pm, Sun 1–6pm; Oct–May
Mon–Fri 10.30am–4.30pm, Sat & Sun 1–6pm; adult €4, children
€2.

Fort Dunree began life as a Martello tower during the
Napoleonic Wars and was erected very near the spot where
one of the leaders of the 1798 Rebellion, Wolfe Tone, was
brought ashore. The fort was extensively enlarged during the
late nineteenth century and nowadays houses a collection of
military memorabilia, somewhat enlivened by interactive displays. The old fort hospital now holds an exhibition devoted
to local wildlife and their habitats.

## Father McDyer's Folk Village Museum

Glencolmcille; ☎ 074/973 0017. Easter–Sept Mon–Sat
10am–6pm, Sun noon–6pm; adults €2.75, children €2, family
€9.50.

Named in honour of a priest who helped to catalyse an eco-
nomic revival in the area during the 1950s, this museum consists of a cluster of replica thatched buildings furnished
according to the fashions of the 1700s, 1800s and early 1900s,
and offering the chance to see how our ancestors might have
lived. The reception building features displays of the area's
history and heritage and there's also a replica of a National
School and a shebeen house where you can enjoy delights
such as seaweed wine. There's also a tea house here with its
own bakery and a craft shop (oh, and the beach is just over
the dunes by the edge of the car park).

## St Connell's Museum and Heritage Centre

Glenties; ☎ 074/955 1227. June–Sept Mon–Sat 10am–1pm, Sun
2–4.30pm; adults €2.50, children €1.

Occupying the old Courthouse, this small museum packs a
host of information into every available space. Inside you'll
find displays on local wildlife, music, antiquities, Donegal railways, household artefacts, antique toys and the effects of the
Great Famine, including a famine pot from the Glenties
workhouse. The basement houses the building's former cells,
as well as re-creations of a schoolroom, kitchen and forge.

## Inishowen Maritime Museum and
Planetarium

Old Coastguard Station, Greencastle; ☎ 074/938 1363,
ⓦ www.inishowenmaritime.com; Easter–Sept Mon–Sat
10am–6pm, Sun noon–6pm; Oct–Easter Mon–Fri 10am–5pm;
museum: adults €4, children €2, family €10; museum & planetarium: adults €8, children €4, family €20.

If you love boats and the sea, you'll thoroughly enjoy the range of exhibits housed in the Maritime Museum, ranging from memorabilia and ancient seafaring equipment to a fully-rigged "Greencastle yawl" (a traditional fishing boat) to a wildfowling punt with a swivel gun and a nineteenth-century rocket-driven cart. The Planetarium allows visitors to view the stars on any historical date and see how the skies have changed over the last two thousand years. Lastly, there are special Laser Light concerts on various summer evenings, featuring a thrilling and dynamic laser system linked to a wide range of music, from traditional to Led Zeppelin.

## Ionad Cois Locha/The Dunlewey Lakeside Centre

Dunlewey Lough, Gweedore; ☎ 074/953 1699; ⓦ www.dunlewey-centre.com; Easter–Oct, Mon–Sat 10.30am–6pm, Sun 11–6pm; cottage tour or boat trip: adults €5, children €3.50, family €12.50; combined cottage tour and boat trip: adults €8, children €6, family €20; adventure play area: adults €3.50, children €3, family €10.

Right next to the stunningly beautiful Dunlewey Lough, this centre incorporates a a craft, book and CD shop as well as a popular restaurant. Outside there are restored farm buildings, including a farm museum and plenty of more recently arrived farm animals, together with a re-creation of the home of a local weaver. The adventure play area has its own artificial lake and also activities under cover for rainy days, but best of all is the boat trip on the Lough complete with storyteller. The centre also hosts the Trad Trathnóna series of traditional music concerts on Tuesday evenings and occasional other nights during the summer months.

## Fintown Railway

Fintown; ☎ 074/954 6128. July–Sept daily 2–7pm; adults €3, children €1, family €8.

Donegal once had some two hundred miles of railways, but the only part now in use is a small section running for one and a half miles along the shore of Lough Finn. It's a gorgeous setting and taking a ride along the narrow gauge track is a thoroughly enjoyable experience.

## Glenveagh National Park and Castle

Churchill, Letterkenny; ☎ 074/913 7090, ⓦ www.heritageireland.ie; Mid-March–early Nov, daily 10am–6.30pm; park: adults €2.75, children €1.25, family €7, castle: adults €2.75, children €1.25, family €7. Heritage card.

Entered via the R251, several miles north of Churchill, the National Park incorporates much of the Derryveagh Mountains. Splendid walking country but it's the castle, overlooking Lough Beagh, which attracts most visitors. The Park's visitor centre provides very detailed, interactive displays on local wildlife and geology and, from here, there's a free minibus ride along the lough shore to the castle itself. Before taking the guided tour be sure to climb through the gardens to absorb the fabulous view of the lough and surrounding countryside.

## Letterkenny Karting Centre

Ballymaleel, Letterkenny; ⓣ 074/912 9077. Mon–Sat,1–10.30pm.
Take a kart for a spin on a track more than 900 yards long, race against others (the track can cater for twenty competitors at one time) or just practise your skills. Prices start from €10 for a ten-minute ride.

## Newmills Corn and Flax Mills

Churchill Rd, Letterkenny; ⓣ 074/912 5115, ⓦ www.heritageireland.ie; June–Sept, daily 10am–6.30pm; adults €2.75, children €1.25, family €7. Heritage card.
The oldest building in this complex of mills dates back some four hundred years and it was only as recently as 1982 that the mills stopped operating commercially. Fortunately, much of the machinery is still in use and there's the chance to watch it in operation, powered by the River Swilly turning its massive water wheel, one of the largest in Ireland.

## The Old Courthouse

The Diamond, Lifford; ⓣ 074/914 1733,
ⓦ www.infowing.ie/seatofpower. Mon–Fri 9am–4.30pm, Sun 12.30–4pm; adults €5, children €2.50, family €12.50.
Visiting this prestigious old building, which dates back to 1746, you'll find yourself witnessing enjoyable re-enactments of famous trials (including that of the 1798 rebel Napper Tandy) before being whisked down to the original dungeons where you'll be taken into custody, charged and fingerprinted. Fortunately you can avoid a lengthy incarceration and visit the onsite restaurant to consume more pleasant fare than the typical penal diet.

## Doon Fort

Narin; open access.
This astonishing fortress occupies all of an oval-shaped islet in the middle of Lough Doon. Though some of its ancient walls are crumbling, most still stand at 15 feet high and 12 feet thick and the inner passages were used to stash poteen in the 1950s. Getting to this tranquil setting can be difficult, but, driving from Ardara to Narin, turn left at the

Rosbeg/Tramore Beach signpost a mile before Narin, then next head right up the lane shortly after the school. After a few hundred yards you'll spot a "boat rental" sign pointing down to a farmhouse where you can rent a rowing boat for €3, taking you into a "Famous Five"-type adventure that all the family should enjoy.

## Flight of the Earls Heritage Centre

Rathmullan; ☎ 074/915 8131, ⓦ www.flightoftheearls.com; June–Sept, Mon–Sat 10am–6pm, Sun 12.30–6pm; Oct–May Mon–Sat 10am–1pm & 2–5pm, Sun 11am–3pm; adults €5, children €2.

Housed in a fort built by the British in 1810 as defence against a feared French invasion, the loughside centre focuses on the 1607 Flight of the Earls (a key moment in Irish history) and, particularly, the O'Donnell and O'Neill chieftains. Displays and exhibits set the Flight's historical background and explain the Plantation of Ulster, describing the exploits of prominent local families and incorporating hanging fabrics to re-create the atmosphere of sixteenth-century Gaelic court life. Those who want to see the exact spot from which the Earls are believed to have departed should head to the slipway at Portnamurry, three-quarters of a mile towards Ramelton.

## Leisureland

Redcastle; ☎ 074/938 2306, ⓦ www.leisurelandredcastle.ie; Easter–Sept, Sat & Sun noon–7.30pm; June–Aug, Mon–Fri noon–6pm; charges for various amusements.

Situated off the R238 Muff–Moville road, Leisureland is an indoor amusement centre offering a range of rides and activities for ages 3–14. Amongst the attractions are a pirate ship, safari train, eight-ball pool and carousel, or you can test your driving skills out on the dodgems and F1 cars and beat opponents at air hockey. All activities are supervised and there's also a fast-food restaurant here.

## Slieve League

Bunglass, Teelin; open access.

Reckoned to be the tallest of their kind in Europe, the marine cliffs of Slieve League are one of the most thrilling sights in the whole country. To get there, follow the signs out of Teelin to the car park at Bunglass and be warned that the road takes you along sharp bends and up vertiginous inclines. At Bunglass you can view the two-thousand-foot cliff face in all its glory, its mineral deposits sparkling in the sun as the sea crashes below. Older children will also be capable of taking the path up to the cliff top for a spectacular view of the waters below and, it's reckoned on a good day, up to a third of Ireland. Another way of viewing the cliffs is to take a boat trip from Teelin on the Nuala Star (℡ 074/973 9365, Ⓦ www.nwcsa.com/nualasta; call for times and prices).

# Sports and activities

## Adventure and activity centres

**Donegal Adventure Centre**, Dinglei Coush, Bundoran, ℡ 071/984 2418, Ⓦ www.donegal-holidays.com; **Gartan Outdoor Education Centre**, Churchill, Letterkenny, ℡ 074/913 7032, Ⓦ www.gartan.com; **Irishadventure.com**, Hillhead, Ardara, ℡ 074/954 1100, Ⓦ www.irishadventure.com; **Malinmore Adventure Centre**, Malinmore, ℡ 074/973 0006.

## Bicycle rental

**Bikes and Toys**, Carndonagh, ℡ 074/937 4084; **Don Byrne,** West End, Ardara, ℡ 074/954 1658; **O'Doherty's**, Main St, Donegal town, ℡ 074/972 1119.

## Cinemas

**The Abbey Centre**, Market St, Ballyshannon, ℡ 071/985 1375; **Bundoran Cineplex**, Station Rd, Bundoran, ℡ 071/982 9999; **Century Cinemas**, Leckview Lane, Pearse Rd, Letterkenny, ℡ 074/912 5050; **Lifford Strabane Cineplex**, Lifford, ℡ 074/914 1963, Ⓦ www.liffordstrabane.com;

## Horseriding

**Ashtree Stables**, Coole, Cranford, ℡ 074/915 3312; **Carrigart Riding Centre**, Wood Quarter, Cranford, ℡ 074/915 3583; **Castle View Farm,** Kilcashe, Loughros Point, ℡ 074/954 1212; **Dunfanaghy Riding Stables**, Arnolds Hotel, Dunfanaghy, ℡ 074/913 6208, Ⓦ www.arnoldshotel.com; **Golden Sands Equestrian Centre**, Rathmullan, ℡ 074/915 8124; **Homefield Equestrian Centre**, Bayview Ave, West End, Bundoran, ℡ 071/984 1288); **Inch Island Stables**, Inch Island, Burnfoot, ℡ 074/936 0335; **Lenamore Stables**, Muff, ℡ 074/938 4022, Ⓦ www.lenamorestables.com

## Pitch and Putt

**Letterkenny Pitch 'n' Putt**, Ramelton Rd, Letterkenny, ℡ 074/912 5688; **Sandfield Pitch and Putt**, Narin Rd, Ardara, ℡ 074/954 1344.

## Swimming

**Waterworld**, Seafront, Bundoran; ☏ 071/984 1172, ⓦ www.water-worldbundoran.com; Easter week, May and Sept Sat & Sun, June–Aug daily 10am–7pm; adults e7.50, children under 8 e5, under 3 e3. This massively popular indoor complex features two leisure pools, flumes, a wave pool with rapids and, most thrilling of all, the ultra-speedy "whizzer" slide. Also here are the Aqua Maris seaweed baths which offer adults the chance to wallow in the invigorating green "soup".

# Accommodation

**Greene's Holiday Hostel**, Carnmore Rd, Dungloe; ☏ 074/952 1943. Well-equipped hostel with family rooms from €14 per person, bike rental and camping.

**Highlands Hotel**. Glenties; ☏ 074/955 1111, ⓦ ww.highland-shotel.com; Family-run and family-welcoming, the Highland is a very comfortable establishment, also offering superb-value bar and a la carte meals; from €46 per person with child reductions.

**Shandon Hotel and Leisure Centre**, Marble Hill Strand, Sheephaven Bay, Dunfanaghy; ☏ 074/913 6317, ⓦ www.shan-donhotel.com; Not so much a very relaxing hotel, but a child-friendly entertainment centre, featuring swimming pool, basketball court and indoor play area, July & Aug only); from €73 per night with children at €8–€67 depending on age.

**Trean House**, Tremone, Lecamy; ☏ 074/916 7121, ⓦ www.trean-house.com; This very comfortable seaside farmhouse B&B is an enjoyable base for exploring Inishowen; family room and twin, from €24.50 per person with child reductions.

# Places to eat

**Leo's Tavern**, Meenaleck. Home pub of the band Clannad, the newly-rebuilt Leo's is a very popular place for families, not least for its superb fish and chips.

**Nancy's**, Front St, Ardara. An atmospheric local serving a mouth-watering range of bar meals and snacks.

**Sweeny's White Horse**, Bundoran Rd, Ballyshannon. Excellent bar serving an imaginative menu.

**Teach Bearnaí**, Main St, Kilcar; ☏ 074/973 8160. Very welcoming restaurant serving fine evening meals and Sunday lunches.

**The Water's Edge**, Rathmullan; ☏ 074/915 8182. This loughside restaurant's range of cuisine is really hard to beat and certainly the place to come for a treat.

# 14

# Belfast

As Northern Ireland's largest city, Belfast will be remembered as the focus of the continuing political disputes which have dominated so many people's lives since 1969. However, this one-time centre of shipbuilding and the linen trade is remarkably changed. Though there are still occasional flashpoints, the

## Information

**The Belfast Welcome Centre** 47 Donegall Place (Mon–Sat
9am–5.30pm; ☎ 028/9024 6609, ⓦ www.gotobelfast.com)
stocks information about an enormous range of events and
attractions in Belfast and throughout the whole of Northern
Ireland. *Whatabout?* is a monthly free magazine, available from
the Belfast Welcome Centre, providing detailed listings of entertainment, festivals, exhibitions and visitor attractions; it also
includes its own "family fun" section. Also be sure to pick up a
copy of *NI4Kids* (ⓦ www.ni4kids.com) a bi-monthly free newspa-
per entirely devoted to children's events and activities in
Northern Ireland.

security presence is virtually invisible, making it a very safe
place for tourists, and the city's docklands and other areas have
witnessed extensive reinvigoration. There are plenty of things
for families to see and do here and Belfast's arts and nightlife
are as good as you'll find in any major European city.

## Aunt Sandra's Candy Factory

60 Castlereagh Rd; ☎ 028/9073 2868,
ⓦ www.irishcandyfactory.com; Mon–Fri 9.30am–4.30pm, Sat
9.30am–5pm; free (advance booking essential).
A re-creation of the original 1953 shop, complete with
wooden ceilings and slate floors, Aunt Sandra's offers visitors
the chance to watch the handmade manufacture of a range of
chocolates and candies and to sample delights such as hum-
bugs and traditional fudge.

## Belfast Zoo

off Antrim Rd; ☎ 028/9077 6277, ⓦ www.belfastzoo.co.uk; daily
10am–5pm (Oct–March 10am–2.30pm); April–Sept adults £6.40,
children £3.20, family £17.50; Oct–March adults £5.40, children
£2.70, family £14.50.
Spread over landscaped parkland, the zoo houses more than one
hundred and sixty species of rare and endangered animals and
focuses firmly upon conservation and education. There's a host of
monkeys, plenty of big cats, lemurs, giraffes, tapirs and sea lions,
alongside many wildfowl and a walkthrough aviary, but the biggest
draw is probably the meerkats who live in the African enclosure.

## Cave Hill Country Park and Belfast Castle

Antrim Rd. Daily dawn–dusk; free.
Cave Hill dominated the Belfast skyline north of the city and
takes its name from the Neolithic caves which puncture its
cliffs. Thanks to its shape in silhouette form the hill acquired
the nickname "Napoleon's Nose" in the nineteenth century

# BELFAST

Carrickfergus, Larne, Derry & Belfast Int. Airport

Belfast City Airport, Cultra & Bangor

Stormont & Newtownards

Larne, Belfast Castle, Cave Hill, Zoo, Crumlin & Belfast Int. Airport

Lisburn

Lisburn, Newry & Dublin

Norse Irish Ferry Terminal

Herdman Channel

Victoria Channel

Musgrave Channel

Victoria Park

Dunmore Park

YORK ROAD

YORK STREET

MOTORWAY M2

York Road Rail Station

Stena Ferry Terminal

SYDENHAM BYPASS

Seacat & I.O.M. Ferry Terminal

Freedom Corner

NEWTOWNARDS ROAD

Odyssey Complex

Queen Elizabeth Bridge

Queen's Bridge

ALBERT BRIDGE RD

ANTRIM ROAD

CLIFTON STREET

Belfast Cathedral

DONEGALL

NORTH

ST

ST

Bus Station

Waterfront Hall

SHORT STRAND

ALBERT BRIDGE

Crumlin Road Gaol

OXFORD ST

Central Station

SHANKILL ROAD

ROYAL AVE

HIGH ST

STREET

CASTLE ST

City Hall

DIVIS ST

BBC

Conway Mill

GROSVENOR ROAD

GT VICTORIA ST

DUBLIN ROAD

ORMEAU AVE

FALLS RD

St. Peter's Cathedral

Great Victoria St Station & Bus Station

Botanic Rail Station

Ormeau Park

Ormeau Bridge

WESTLINK

DONEGALL

ROAD

Queen's Film Theatre

Royal Victoria Hospital

Queen's University

Ulster Museum

STRANMILLIS ROAD

Botanic Gardens

King's Bridge

FALLS RD

Cultúrlann MacAdam Ó Fiaich

UNIVERSITY

STRANMILLIS

RD

STRANMILLIS EMBANKMENT

Lyric Theatre

Governor's Bridge

ADELAIDE PARK

LISBURN ROAD

MALONE ROAD

STRANMILLIS ROAD

Milltown Cemetery

MOTORWAY M1

N

MALONE

King's Hall

0        500 yds

BELFAST CITY CENTRE  119

because of its resemblance to the Emperor of France's physiognomy. The park is a haven for many forms of wildlife and a hunting ground, too, for birds of prey such as kestrels. There are also three waymarked trails, the longest of which (at 4 miles) passes the caves on the way to the viewpoint of McArt's Fort, while the shortest passes the Adventurous Playground (suitable for 3–14 year olds, ☎ 028/9037 1013 for opening times and prices) and the Millennium Maze (free). In the centre of the park stands Belfast Castle which houses the Cave Hill Visitor Centre (Mon–Sat 9am–10.30pm, Sun 9am–6pm; free; ☎ 028/9077 6925, ⓦ www.belfastcastle.co.uk; free) which recounts the history of the area from the Stone Age to modern times. The park also houses Belfast Zoo (above).

## Colin Glen Forest Park

Stewartstown Rd; ☎ 028/9061 4115, ⓦ www.colinglen.org; daily dawn–dusk; free.

Five miles west of the city centre, the forest park consists of 200 acres of mixed woodland and grassland set around an attractive river glen. In addition to its waterfalls and ponds, the park provides a programme of guided walks during the summer months (including a Bluebell Walk and the fossil-collecting Dinosaur Walk) plus an environmental week in August and Bat Nights (hunts for the flying mammals in the forest). Activities usually cost £2 for adults and £1 for children and all children must be accompanied.

## Lagan Lookout Centre

Donegall Quay; ☎ 028/9031 5444, ⓦ www.laganside.com; April–Sept, Mon–Fri 11am–5pm, Sat noon–5pm, Sun 2–5pm; Oct–March Tues–Fri 11am–3.30pm, Sat 1–4.30pm, Sun 2–4.30pm; adults £1.50, children £0.75, family £4

Designed to protect Belfast from flooding, the Lagan weir was the first completed component of the continuing river and docks redevelopment project. The raised, circular Lookout Centre explains the details of the weir project and explores the river's vital role in the development of such diverse industries as linen, rope-making and shipbuilding. Carefully positioned windows around the centre point out Belfast landmarks.

## Lagan Valley Regional Park

South Belfast to Lisburn; ☎ 028/9049 1922. Mostly open access; free.

The Regional Park is actually a connected network of urban and countryside parks, heritage sites, nature reserves and riverside trails, extending for eleven miles along both sides of the River Lagan between the south Belfast suburb of Stranmillis and the Upper Locks at Lisburn, Co. Antrim. Its attractions include nineteenth-century Malone House, Upper Malone Rd (Mon–Sat 10am–4.30pm; free; ☎ 028/9068 1246, Ⓦ www.malonehouse.co.uk), set in exquisite parkland (daily dawn–dusk) which has a fine restaurant and an art gallery occasionally featuring exhibitions of interest to children. Further south, past Shaw's Bridge, is the Giant's Ring (daily dawn–dusk; free), a massive prehistoric earthwork, over 200 yards in diameter, which has a dolmen at its centre.

The Regional Park's events programme runs from April to October and includes activities such as the "pond dip" (exploring life in freshwater ponds), guided rambles, discovery mornings and the butterfly discovery trail. All activities are free, but advance booking is essential for the majority.

## Sheridan IMAX Cinema

Odyssey Pavilion, 2 Queen's Quay; ☎ 028/9046 7000 for times of shows, Ⓦ www.belfastimax.com; £4.50 per person.

Featuring a screen ten times larger than a normal cinema (and taller than four double-decker buses stacked on top of each other) and a 12,000 watt digital surround-sound system, the cinema offers two-dimensional large format and 3-D screenings. Films include the ocean-exploring *Into the Deep*, the mountain-climbing *Everest, T-Rex: Back to the Crustaceans* and the witty *Encounter in the Third Dimension*.

## Streamvale Open Farm

38 Ballyhanwood Rd, Gilnahirk; ☎ 028/9048 3244, Ⓦ www.streamvale.co.uk; Feb–May & Sept–Oct, Weds, Sat & Sun 2–6pm; June, Mon–Sat noon–6pm, Sun 2–6pm; July–Aug Mon–Sat 10.30am–6pm, Sun 2–6pm; adults £3.95, children £3.50, family £13.50.

Situated off Old Dundonald Road in East Belfast (just past the International Ice Bowl, see p.123), this family-run, working dairy farm offers children the chance to take part in animal feeding, pony and tractor rides, visits to the milking parlour, a mouse farm and a nature trail.

## The Ulster Museum

Stranmillis Rd; ☎ 028/9038 3000, Ⓦ www.ulstermuseum.org. Mon–Fri 10am–5pm, Sat 1–5pm, Sun 2–5pm; free.

Much of the museum's massive collection has been displayed with children in mind and there's plenty here to entice and enjoy. The ground floor houses both a gallery of replica dinosaur skeletons and fully operational monsters from the age of industrialisation, including a massive vertical steam engine, a loom and water wheels. Upstairs there's a fascinating "Made in Belfast" exhibition examining the wide productive range of the city's industries, and the hugely enjoyable Early Ireland gallery which traces the development of the prehistoric population. The museum has an excellent café and runs a "Back Pack Trail" on the last Sunday of every month (except December) providing free activity packs containing exercises and activities colour-coded to suit different ages.

## Whowhatwherewhenwhy (W5)

Odyssey Pavilion, 2 Queen's Quay; ☏ 028/9046 7700, ⓦ www.w5online.co.uk; Mon–Sat 10am–6pm, Sun noon–6pm; adults £5.50, children £3.50.

Known as W5, this huge and vastly entertaining interactive scientific discovery centre is one of Belfast's most popular attractions and has almost 150 different exhibits crammed into five areas – WOW, START, GO, SEE and DO. Activities range from creating your own animated cartoon to operating a lie detector via testing your compositional skills on a laser harp. The centre operates an extensive programme of additional events and activities, especially during the school holidays, featuring regularly changing exhibitions and live science demonstrations, and now also houses an excellent new photographic gallery.

# Sports and activities

## Bicycle rental

**Life Cycles**, 36–37 Smithfield Market; ☏ 028/9043 9959, ⓦ www.lifecycles.co.uk;

## Boat trips

**The Lagan Boat Company;** ☏ 028/9024 6609, ⓦ www.laganboat-company.com; Operates a seventy-five minute cruise down the river from the Lagan Lookout Centre to Cutter's Wharf, Stranmillis and a one hour *Titanic Tour* around the docks from the landing stage opposite the Royal Mail building (also picking up passengers at the jetty by Odyssey Pavilion); call for times, adults £5, children £4 per tour.

## Cinemas

**Belfast Cineplex**, Kennedy Centre, Falls Rd, ☏ 028/9060 0988; **Movie House**, Yorkgate, ☏ 028/9075 5000, ⓦ www.moviehouse.co.uk; **UGC**, Dublin Rd, ☏ 0870/155 5176, ⓦ www.ugcccinemas.co.uk; **Warner Village**, Odyssey Pavilion, ☏ 0870/240 6020, ⓦ www.warnervillage.co.uk;

## Gaelic football, hurling and camogie

Matches take place on Sunday afternoons at Casement Park,

Andersonstown (☎ 028/9038 3815 for details).

## Swimming

**Grove Leisure Centre** York Rd, ☎ 028/9035 1599; **Maysfield Leisure Centre**, East Bridge St, ☎ 028/9024 1633; **Olympia Leisure Centre**, Boucher Rd, ☎ 028/9023 3369; **Shankill Leisure Centre**, Shankill Rd, ☎ 028/9024 1434.

## Ten pin bowling

**Dundonald International Ice Bowl** (see above); **Euphoria,** Odyssey Pavilion, 2 Queen's Quay; ☎ 028/9046 7030, ⓦ www.euphoriabelfast.com;

# Accommodation

**Greenwood Guest House,** 25 Park Rd; ☎ 028/9020 2525, ⓦ www.greenwoodguesthouse.com; Pleasant, family-run B&B situated next to Ormeau Park, offering bright and airy rooms and reductions for children sharing; from £27.50 per person.
**Holiday Inn**, Ormeau Ave; ☎ 0870/400 9005, ⓦ www.belfast.holiday-inn.com; Modern hotel offering stunning rooms and breakfasts and great family deals from £32 per person (under-12s free).
**Jurys Inn Belfast**, Fisherwick Place, Great Victoria St; ☎ 028/9053 3500, ⓦ www.jurysdoyle.com; Offers a prime city centre location and an all-in room-rate from £71,
**Malone Lodge Hotel**, 60 Eglantine Ave; ☎ 028/9038 8000, ⓦ www.malonelodgehotel.com; Very comfortable hotel near the University, offering well-equipped rooms and weekend breaks from £39.50 per person with reductions for children sharing.

# Places to eat

**Hard Rock Café**, Odyssey Pavilion, 2 Queen's Quay; ☎ 028/9076 6990. Extensive American-style menu and walls bedecked with assorted rock music memorabilia; daily noon–late.
**Maggie May's**, 45 Botanic Ave; ☎ 028/9032 2662. Wholesome Irish cooking served with plenty of vegetarian choices, daily from 7.45am–11pm.
**The Morning Star**, 17–19 Pottinger's Entry. Old coaching inn, serving a splendid help-yourself lunchtime buffet and a more extensive á la carte menu upstairs.
**Villa Italia**, 37–41 University Rd; ☎ 028/9032 8356. Long-stand-

# 15

# Antrim and Derry

Antrim is the Northern Irish county most visited by tourists. Its splendid coast road from Larne heads northwards alongside the celebrated nine Glens of Antrim, taking in marvellous sea views on the way to Cushendall and Ballycastle before passing two major attractions, the Carrick-a-Rede rope bridge and

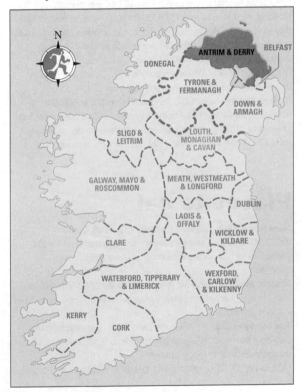

the Giant's Causeway, ad reaching the lively seaside resort of Portrush. Derry city is the main magnet in the county of the same name, a bustling place with an ever-lively arts scene.

## Brookhall Historical Farm

2 Horse Park, Ballinderry, Co. Antrim; ☎028/9262 1712; Easter–Oct Wed–Sat 11am–5pm. Sun 2–6pm; adults £2, children £1.

Some four miles west of Lisburn, this attractive open farm features plenty of rare breeds, a duck pond, pleasant gardens and a farming museum devoted to a collection of bygone agricultural equipment.

## Carrick-a-Rede Rope Bridge

Ballintoy, Co. Antrim; ☎ 028/2073 1159, ⓦ www.ntni.org.uk; mid-March–June & Sept, daily 10am–6pm; July–Aug, daily 9.30am–7.30pm; free, car parking £3.50; National Trust.

Take a walk from the main land across this swinging, bouncing sixty-foot rope bridge (guaranteed to raise whoops and screams from the bravest souls) crossing an almost eighty feet deep chasm to Carrick-a-Rede which means literally "the rock in the road", a very popular spot for salmon fishing. The rope bridge is a mile from the car park along a cliff path and is only open when weather conditions are safe.

## Watertop Open Farm

188 Cushendall Rd, nr. Ballypatrick Forest Park, Co. Antrim; ☎ 028/2076 2576, ⓦ www.watertopfarm.co.uk; July–Aug, daily 11am–5.30pm; adults £2, children £1.

Some five miles southeast of Ballycastle on the A2, Watertop offers farm tours, including the chance to watch a demonstration of shearing, and activities such as pony trekking, fishing and boating (all at extra charge), as well as scenic walks. There's a restaurant too and a pleasant campsite (open April–Oct).

# ECOS Millennium Environmental Centre

Kernohans Lane, Broughshane Rd, Ballymena, Co. Antrim;
☎ 028/2566 4400, Ⓦ www.ecoscentre.com; Easter–Sept
Mon–Sat 10.30am–5pm, Sun noon–5pm; Oct–Easter Mon–Sat
noon–4pm; adults £4, children £3, under-4s free, family £12.50.
ECOS is a recently constructed centre, set in a 150-acre park,
which successfully educates on environmental issues through a
variety of entertaining and participatory activities. Indoors,
children can build their own simulations of rainforests, watch
the speed at which a car generates its own weight in $CO_2$ and
learn how to reduce waste and reuse and recycle what remains.
Outside, the park houses a host of butterflies, dragonflies, birds
and wild flowers. The centre organizes regular events such as
pond-dipping and guided rambles and runs Saturday and
Sunday afternoon workshops on a variety of enjoyable topics.

## Leslie Hill Open Farm

Macfin Rd, Ballymoney, Co. Antrim; ☎028/2766 6803. Easter–May,
Sun 2–6pm; June, Sat & Sun 2–6pm; July & Aug, Mon–Sat 11–6pm,
Sun 2–6pm; adults £2.90, children £1.90, family £8.50.
Home to ten generations of the Leslie family, the farm provides the chance to explore its buildings, machinery, carriages
and carts and to meet a friendly collection of birds and animals, including a herd of red deer. There's also a pleasant
walled garden, walks through wooded parkland, a tearoom
and the chance to ride around the farm in an open wagon.

## Carrickfergus Castle

Marine Highway, Carrickfergus, Co. Antrim; ☎ 028/9335 1273,
Ⓦ www.ehsni.gov.uk; April–Sept, Mon–Sat 10am–6pm, Sun
2–6pm, (June–Aug noon–6pm); Oct–March Mon–Sat 10am–4pm,
Sun 2–4pm; adults £3, children £1.50, family £8.
Overlooking the harbour, the castle was begun in around
1180 by the Anglo-Norman invader John de Courcy and
remained a military bastion for much of its succeeding life (it
was garrisoned until 1928). Tour guides direct you around the
castle, recounting key events in its history and introducing
you to the life-size models of some of its key characters –
you can meet de Courcy and his wife Lady Affreca in the
inner courtyard. The castle is the venue for the medieval
Lughnasa Fayre on the last Saturday in July.

## Flame – The Gasworks Museum of Ireland

44 Irish Quarter West, Carrickfergus, Co. Antrim; ☎ 028/9336
9575, Ⓦ www.gasworksflame.com. March & Oct, Sat & Sun
2–6pm, April, June & Sept, daily 2–6pm; July & Aug, daily
10am–6pm; £2 per person.
Ireland's only surviving coal-fired gasworks was built between

1855 and 1867 to light Carrickfergus's street lamps and operated until 1964 (the Big Lamp at the end of the High Street is
one of the few survivors). The gasworks has been restored by
enthusiasts and now provides a diverting account of its former
functions. There's also the chance to climb up to the top of
the gasholder and enjoy a fine view of the town below.

## T.A.C.T. Wildlife Centre

2 Crumlin Rd, Crumlin, Co. Antrim; ℗ 028/9445 9739,
Ⓦ www.tactwildlifecentre.org.uk; Mon–Fri noon–3pm, Sun
2–5pm; suggested donation adults £3, children £1.50.
The Talnotry Avian Care Trust looks after sick, injured and
abandoned birds and small mammals, preparing them for a
return to the wild whenever possible. Long-term residents on
view include owls, falcons, gannets, foxes, rabbits and hedge-
hogs.

## Carnfunnock Country Park

Drains Bay, Coast Rd, Larne, Co. Antrim; ℗ 028/2827,
℗ 028/2827 0541, Ⓦ www.larne.gov.uk; dawn–dusk; car parking
charge related to length of visit.
Some three miles north of Larne, Carnfunnock is a delightful
country park offering plenty to suit children of all ages. As
well as a maze in the shape of Northern Ireland, there's a
walled garden featuring a variety of sundials, a children's
activity centre (including an outdoor adventure playground),
plenty of forest walks and rides on a miniature railway
(Easter–October). The park hosts an extensive programme of
events including birds of prey displays, Easter egg hunts, sto-
rytelling and a horse and pony show. There's also a nine-hole
golf course and a coffee shop.

## Irish Linen Centre and Lisburn Museum

Market Square, Lisburn, Co. Antrim; ℗ 028/9266 3377,
Ⓦ www.lisburn.gov.uk; Mon–Sat 9.30am–5pm; free.
The museum's permanent exhibition, Flax to Fabric, recounts
the history of Northern Ireland's linen industry and includes
weavers plying their craft on purpose-built hand looms. The
rest of the space houses temporary exhibitions and the building's modern annexe is home to the local tourist office.

## Giant's Causeway

Causeway Head, Co. Antrim; open access. Giant's Causeway
visitor centre; ℗ 028/2073 1855, Ⓦ www.northantrim.com: daily
June 10am–6pm, July–Aug 10am–7pm, Sept–May 10am–5pm;
free, car parking £5.
Unquestionably, the Giant's Causeway is the most popular
attraction in Northern Ireland with crowds flocking all year

round to witness the spectacle of this bizarre formation of more than 37,000 black basalt columns, each in the shape of a polygon. So, to avoid the crowds, it's best to arrive early in the morning or late in the afternoon. The best approach to the Causeway is the cliff-top path accessed from behind the Visitor Centre and then taking the steps down to the beach below. Alternatively, you can follow the road down the hill from the Centre or take a minibus (£1.20 return per person). Once there you can marvel at the somewhat unworldly scene and wonder whether the legendary giant Finn McCool really did build the Causeway either to visit an inamorata or beat up another giant in Scotland. Getting to the Causeway couldn't be easier. There's the narrow gauge railway from Bushmills (Ⓣ028/2073 2844, Ⓦwww.giantscausewayrailway.org. March, April & Oct Sat & Sun 11am–4pm; May–Sept daily 11am–5pm; adults' return fare £5, children £3, family £14) or the regular "open topper" bus running daily in July and August from Coleraine and stopping at Portstewart, Portrush and Bushmills along the way.

## Causeway School Museum

Beside Giant's Causeway Centre, Co. Antrim; Ⓣ 028/2073 1777; July–Aug, daily 11am–5pm; adults £0.75, children £0.50, family £2.

Situated at the end of the Causeway Centre car park the school, which functioned from 1915 to 1962, was designed by Clough Williams Ellis (famed architect of Portmeirion in Wales). The museum houses displays on the school's history while a video re-creates a day in its life during the 1920s. Children can attempt copperplate handwriting and experiment with some bygone pastimes such as spinning tops.

## Glenariff Forest Park

Glenariff, Co. Antrim; Ⓣ 028/2955 6000, Ⓦ www.forestserviceni.gov.uk. Daily 9am–dusk; car £3, adult pedestrian £1.50, child pedestrian £0.50.

Up in the hills above the village of Waterfoot lies this splendid forest park, renowned for its marvellous walks around the glen to mountain viewpoints. The best of these is the waymarked Waterfall Trail which takes you to a stunning series of cascades, whose beauty can be admired from the safety of a timber walkway. There's a campsite and space for touring caravans.

## Ford Farm Park and Museum

8 Low Rd, Islandmagee, Co. Antrim; Ⓣ 028/9335 3264, Ⓦ www.ford-farm.co.uk; March–Oct daily 2–6pm; adults £2.75, children £2.50.

This working farm by the shores of Larne Lough features all manner of animals and offers demonstrations of butter-making and spinning. There's also a small museum here whose many items convey an impression of what life must have been like for farming communities in the past.

## Barry's Amusements

16 Eglinton St, Portush, Co. Antrim; ⊤028/7082 2340, Ⓦwww.barrysamusements.com; Easter–June, Sat 1–10.30pm, Sun 11–10.30pm; July–Aug, daily 1–10.30pm.

There's lots of indoor and outdoor fun to be had in this amusement park with rides including dodgems, cyclone, carousel, ghost train and the frankly stomach-churning looping star (a roller coaster with an upside-down twist) plus plenty of indoor video games. The park operates a system whereby tokens (50p each) are purchased in advance, each attraction costing between one and four tokens.

## Dunluce Castle

3 miles east of Portrush, Co. Antrim; ⊤028/2073 1938, Ⓦwww.ehsni.gov.uk; April–Sept, Mon–Sat 10am–6pm, Sun 2–6pm (June–Aug noon–6pm); Oct–March closes 4pm; adults £2, children £1.

High on a headland, the ruins of sixteenth-century Dunluce Castle could not have a more dramatic setting. The McDonnells ruled from here and the castle's position was always precarious in both political and physical senses. In 1584 it was the subject of a siege by the English and in 1639 the castle kitchen fell off the cliff during a storm. Unsurprisingly, the McDonnells out not long afterwards and the castle was abandoned, gradually falling into ruin. A tour of the remainder is well worth undertaking, as is the scramble down the cliff to a cave which goes right under the headland and has an opening directly under the castle's gatehouse.

## The Dunluce Centre

10 Sandhill Drive, Portrush, Co. Antrim; ⊤ 028/7082 4444, Ⓦ www.touristnetuk.com/ni.dunluce. Easter week, daily 10.30am–7pm; April–May, Sat & Sun noon–7pm; June, Mon–Fri 10am–5pm, Sat & Sun noon–7pm; July–Aug, daily 10.30am–7pm; Sept–March, Sat & Sun noon–5pm; £2.75 per attraction, £7 combined ticket.

The centre houses three attractions resolutely aimed at children. Finn McCool's Adventure Playground includes touch-screen games, an obstacle course, a climbing wall and the delights of a 3D twister. Treasure Fortress is a hi-tech treasure hunt where groups of two or more explore themed castle rooms, solving a quiz trail in order to release a spellbound princess and her fabulous dowry of Spanish treasure. Lastly, Turbo Tours features moving seats synchronized to respond to events in action-packed Hollywood films.

# Portrush Countryside Centre and National Nature Reserve

8 Bath Rd, Portrush, Co. Antrim; ⓣ 028/7082 3600,
ⓦ www.nics.gov.uk/ehs; June–Sept, daily 10am–6pm; free.
While the centre holds an exhibition on the local seashore and marine life, alongside a touch tank and live sea creatures, the adjacent nature reserve offers activities such as fossil hunts, rock pool rambles and birdwatching.

## The Portrush Puffer

Portrush, Co. Antrim; ⓣ 028/7032 5400; July–Aug, every 30min Mon–Sat 11am–1.30pm & 2–7pm, Sun 2–7pm; adults £1.80, children £0.90, family day ticket £5.
This passenger road train plies its way around the town in high season and forms a handy way to enjoy the sites and visit the various attractions.

## Rathlin Island

Co. Antrim.
Northern Island's only inhabited offshore island, lies five off the coast and is easily accessible by ferry from Ballycastle. Caledonian MacBrayne ferries (ⓣ 028/2076 9299, ⓦ www.calmac.co.uk) operate between two and four times daily (adult return £8.40, children £4.20, under-5s free). Once there you can hire a bike from Soerneog View Hostel (ⓣ 028/2076 3954) to tour the island and discover its prehistoric remains or take the regular minibus that runs in summer between Church Bay (the ferry terminal) and Bull Point where the viewpoint at the west lighthouse (April–Aug; contact RSPB warden in advance ⓣ 028/2076 3948) reveals the spectacle of Northern Ireland's largest colony of sea birds, including puffins and guillemots. There's a visitor centre by the harbour (May–Aug daily 10am–4pm; ⓣ 028/2076 3951) and meals are available at The Manor House B&B and McCuaig's bar.

## Patterson's Spade Mill

Templepatrick, Co. Antrim; ⓣ 028/9443 3619, ⓦ www.ntni.org.uk; March, Sun; April–May & Sept, Sat & Sun; June–Aug, daily 2–6pm; adult £3.25, children £1.50, family £8.50; National Trust.
Now here's a strange one. You've almost certainly heard of water-driven corn and flax mills, but this place is the last of its kind in Ireland, a mill that manufactures that well-known gardening implement, the spade! The spade maker takes visitors on a tour of the premises and its still functional hammers, turbine and press and, at the end, will measure you should you wish to buy your own bespoke handcrafted spade.

## Tower Museum

Union Hall Place, Derry city, Co. Derry; ☎ 028/7137 2411,
ⓦ www.derry.net/tower. July–Aug, Mon–Sat 10am–5pm, Sun
2–5pm; Sept–June, Tues–Sat 10am–5pm; adults £3.65, children £2.
Housed in a re-creation of a medieval tower, this excellent
museum provides a detailed and entertaining account of the
city's history employing all manner of tableaux and audiovisual
displays to enrich understanding of key elements in Derry's
development, from early beginnings to the 1688–69 siege and
right up to the Troubles and the present day. At the time of
writing, funding had been obtained for a new gallery focusing
on the treasures of the Spanish Armada.

## Derry City Walls and City centre

The seventeenth-century walls encircling Derry's old city are
amongst the best-preserved defences in Europe and a stroll
along their mile-long walkway forms an essential part of a
visit to the city. The complete circuit takes in all manner of
bulwarks and bastions and four gateways (Shipquay, Ferryquay,
Bishop and Butcher – the gates that were shut during the
famous siege of 1688–89). It passes some of the key sites in
the city's history, such as St Columb's Cathedral, and overlooks
both the Fountain area (a small Protestant enclave) and the
Bogside, a large Nationalist area with its political murals,
Bloody Sunday memorial and Free Derry wall.

## Harbour Museum

Harbour Square, Derry city, Co. Derry; ☎ 028/7137 7331; Mon–Fri
10am–1pm & 2–4.30pm; free.
Well worth a visit for anyone with an interest in maritime history, the museum's most striking exhibits are a replica of the
type of boat in which St Columba is believed to have sailed to
Iona in 563AD and a real longboat found in the River Bann
and dating from the fifteenth century. The museum also hosts
temporary exhibitions.

# Sports and activities

## Adventure and activity centres

**Ardclinis Outdoor Adventure**, High St, Cushendall, Co. Antrim;
☎ 028/2177 1340, ⓦ www.ardclinis.com. Also does bike rental

## Bicycle rental

**Happy Days**, 245 Lone Moor Rd, Derry city, Co. Derry;
☎ 028/7128 7128, ⓦ www.happydays.ie; Ramble Rentals, 28–30
Glenlough, Ballymoney, Co. Antrim, ☎ 028/2766 6676.

## Boat trips

**Ballycastle Charters**, New Pier, Ballycastle, Co. Antrim; ⓣ028/2076 2074. Runs sea-fishing trips during the summer months (Mon, Wed & Fri 7–9pm; adults £10, children £5) and provides free fishing lessons (rod, line and sinker hire £3).

## Cinemas

**Co. Antrim**: Lisburn Omniplex, Governors Rd, Lisburn, ⓣ028/9266 3664; Portrush Playhouse, Main St, Portrush, Co. Antrim, ⓣ028/7082 3917.
**Co. Derry**: Jet Centre, Dunhill Rd, Coleraine, ⓣ028/7032 9909; Orchard Hall, Orchard St, Derry, ⓣ028/7126 2845; Regal, Main St, Limavady, ⓣ028/7776 6158; Strand, Strand Rd, Derry, ⓣ028/7137 3000.

## Go-karting

**Raceview Indoor Karting**, 1 Woodside Rd, Woodside Industrial Estate, Ballymena, Co. Antrim, ⓣ028/2565 1000, ⓦwww.raceviewindoorkarting.co.uk;

## Horseriding

**Co: Antrim**: Castle Hill Equestrian Centre, 86 Fenagh Rd, Ballymena, ⓣ028/2588 1222; Hillmount Equestrian Centre, 6 Straid Rd, Ballycastle, ⓣ028/2076 2686; Islandmagee Riding Centre, 103 Brown's Bay Rd, Islandmagee, ⓣ028/9338 2108, ⓦwww.islandmagee.co.uk; Maddybenny Riding Centre, 11 Maddybenny Park, Portrush, ⓣ028/7082 3394, ⓦwww.maddybenny.freeserve.co.uk; The Rainbow Equestrian Centre, 24 Hollow Rd, Islandmagee, ⓣ028/9338 2929, ⓦwww.activityholsni.co.uk;
**Co. Derry**: Ardmore Stables, 8 Rushall Rd, Ardmore, ⓣ028/7134 5187; Banagher Equestrian Centre, 86 Glenedra Rd, Feeny, ⓣ028/7778 1117; Cool Riding Stables, 68A Ballynahedin Rd, Claudy, ⓣ028/7133 8277; Faughanvale Pony Trekking Centre, 11 Dunedra Rd, Greysteel, ⓣ028/7181 1843 Hill Farm Equestrian Centre, 47 Altikeeragh Rd, Castlerock, ⓣ028/7084 8629; The Island Equestrian Centre, 49 Ballyrashane Rd, Coleraine, ⓣ028/7034 2599; Streeve Hill House, 25 Dowland Rd, Limavady, ⓣ028/7776 6563; Timbertop, Riding Centre, 60 Curran Rd, Aghadowey, ⓣ028/7086 8788.

## Pitch and putt

**Ballyreagh Putting Green**, Portrush, Co. Antrim, ⓣ028/7082 2028; **Curran Park, Larne**, Co. Antrim, ⓣ028/2826 0088; Royal **Portrush Golf Club**, Portrush, Co. Antrim, ⓣ028/7082 2311; **Town Park**, Larne, Co. Antrim, ⓣ028/2826 0478).

## Surfing

The main surfing beaches are at Castlerock and Portstewart, Co. Derry, and Portballintrae and Portush, Co. Antrim, (West Strand, East Strand and White Rocks). A daily surf report is available on ⓣ 0839/337 770 and boards can be rented at several outlets in Portrush and Portstewart. Summer surfing is generally fine, with waves rising to no more than six feet, but can be very dangerous at other times.

## Swimming

**Lagan Valley Leisureplex**, Lisburn Leisure Park, Lisburn, Co. Antrim; ⓣ028/9267 2121, ⓦwww.lisburn.gov.uk. Leisure pool: Mon–Fri 3.30–5.30pm & 6.30–8.30 pm, (Thurs & Fri until 9pm), Sat & Sun 10am–5.30pm; adults £4.60, children £3.20, under-5s free, family £12.80. The North's premier swimming complex, offering competition and diving pools as well as a leisure pool featuring a huge galleon, master-blaster water cannons and tyre rides. Note that the centre is open longer hours during school holidays and that there's a special Lazy River family session each Saturday morning, 10–11am; adults £2.20, children £1.50, under-5s free).

**Waterworld**, The Harbour, Portrush, Co. Antrim; ⓣ028/7082 2001. Easter week and July–Aug, Mon–Sat 10am–8pm, Sun noon–8pm; May & Sept Sat 10am–7pm, Sun noon–7pm; June Mon–Sat 10am–7pm, Sun noon–7pm; £4.50. A fun swimming pool with flumes, slides and power-blasting cannons.

## Tenpin bowling

**Brunswick Superbowl**, Wakehurst Rd, Ballymena, Co.Antrim; ⓣ028/2564 4144, ⓦwww.sportsbowl.com. This has ball walls available to help children score every time and also features an indoor adventure castle, containing a variety of swings and obstacles, plus plenty of video games and a restaurant.

# Accommodation

**Benone Tourist Complex**, 53 Benone Avenue, Benone, Magilligan, Co. Derry; ⓣ028/7755 0555. If you're camping (£7.90 per night) or have a touring caravan or RV (£10.50 per night), Benone is set by a wonderful Blue Flag beach and has heated splash pools, tennis courts, and an adventure play area.

**City Hotel**, Queens Quay, Derry city, Co. Derry; ⓣ028/7136 5800, ⓦwww.greatsouthernhotels.com. Absolutely plush new city centre hotel, offering views of the River Foyle, its own swimming pool and gym and an all-in room rate from £70.

**Maddybenny Farmhouse**, 18 Maddybenny Park, Portrush; ⓣ028/7082 3394, ⓦwww.maddybenny.freeserve.co.uk; Rural farmhouse with superb rooms with great breakfasts from £25 per person (child reductions); also has its own riding centre, a games room and self-catering cottages, sleep 5–8; £300–450 per week).

**The Manor House**, Rathlin Island, Co. Antrim; ⓣ028/2076 2964, ⓦwww.ntni.org.uk. Large, well-equipped guesthouse owned by the National Trust and set right by the waterside; from £23 per person with reductions for children sharing with adults.

**Marine Hotel**, 1 North St, Ballycastle, Co. Antrim; ⓣ028/2076 2222, ⓦwww.marinehotel.net. With sea views and its own indoor swimming pool, the Marine makes a comfortable place to stay; from £37.50 per person with substantial child reductions.

The Saddler's House, 36 Great James St, Derry city, Co. Derry; ⓣ028/7126 9691, ⓦwww.thesaddlershouse.com; Superb city centre B&B both here and at the owners' neighbouring The

# Places to eat

**Bushmills Inn Hotel**, 9 Dunluce Rd, Bushmills, Co, Antrim; ⓣ028/2073 2339. Old coaching inn with turf fires and gas lighting serving splendid bar and restaurant meals and a hugely popular Sunday carvery lunch.

**Harry's**, 10 Mill St, Cushendall, Co. Antrim; ⓣ028/2177 2022. Huge portions and a very extensive menu, including regular daily specials, at this family-friendly bar-restaurant.

**Londonderry Arms Hotel**, 20–28 Harbour Rd, Carnlough, Co. Antrim; ⓣ028/2888 5255. Once owned briefly during the 1920s by Winston Churchill this hotel serves excellent lunches and dinners, including its speciality, Glenarm smoked salmon.

**Morelli's**, 53–58 The Promenade, Portstewart, Co. Derry. Newly-refurbished café serving everything from snacks to full-scale Italian meals with its own justifiably lauded ice cream.

# 16

# Down and Armagh

The neighbouring counties of Down and Armagh occupy the southeastern corner of Northern Ireland. Down is very much a seafaring county, its coastline running east from Belfast, then down the Ards peninsula, almost enclosing the marvellous Strangford Lough, before heading west along Carlingford

Co. Down's tourist offices can be found at: Banbridge, ☎ 028/4062 3322; Bangor, ☎ 028/9127 0069; Downpatrick, ☎ 028/4461 2233; Hillsborough ☎ 028/9268 9717; Kilkeel, ☎ 028/4176 2525; Newcastle, ☎ 028/4372 2222; Newry, ☎ 028/3026 8877; Newtownards, ☎ 028/9182 6846; and Portaferry, ☎ 028/4272 9882.

Co. Armagh's only tourist office is in Armagh city, ☎ 028/3752 1800; though there is an independent South Armagh information office in Crossmaglen, ☎ 028/3086 8900. Details of events and attractions in the county can be found at Ⓦ www.visitarmagh.com and Ⓦ www.south-armagh.com.

Lough to Newry. Not surprisingly, the county has several popular seaside resorts, the best-known being Bangor, Newcastle and Warrenpoint. Between Newcastle and Rostrevor lie the beguiling peaks of the Mourne Mountains and, if you'd like to walk amongst them, it's well worth visiting the Mourne Heritage Trust, 87 Central Promenade (☎ 028/4372 4059; Mon–Fri 9am–5pm) which can advise on the best routes for children. Alternatively, the Mourne Rambler bus takes a circular route through the mountains, starting at Newcastle (☎ 028/4372 2296; July & Aug Mon–Sat 10.10am, 11.35am, 2.05pm, 3.30pm; adults £4, children £2). County Armagh is completely landlocked, but still has plenty of interesting countryside and attractions, the latter not least in the ecclesiastical city of Armagh itself. There's plenty too to see and do around the southern shores of Lough Neagh and in the rural lands surrounding Slieve Gullion in South Armagh.

### Pickie Family Fun Park

The Promenade, Bangor, Co. Down; ☎ 028/9127 4430. March 17 to Oct, daily 9am–dusk; Nov–March 16, Sat & Sun 9am–dusk.

Situated on the western side of Bangor's Marina, the fun park's attractions include pedal boats disguised as swans, a miniature railway, go-karts, a superslide, paddling pools and an adventure playground. Prices range from £1.25 for a train ride to £3 for a pedal boat (seats three).

### Castle Espie Wildfowl and Wetlands Centre

Ballydrain Rd, Comber, Co. Down; ☎ 028/9187 4146, Ⓦ www.wwt.org.uk; March–Oct, Mon–Sat 10.30am–5pm, Sun 11am–5.30pm; Nov–Feb Mon–Fri 11am–4pm, Sat & Sun 11am–4.30pm; adults £4, children £2.50, under 4s free, family £10.50.

Signposted south of Comber on the A22, Castle Espie is home to both native wildfowl and endangered species from other countries which can be viewed from hides, in waterfowl gardens and along woodland walks, allowing children to get "nose to beak" to some of the rarest swans, ducks and geese in the world. In spring and summer there are hundreds of ducklings and flocks of waders and Brent geese arrive in winter. The centre also has an excellent book shop offering further information, a coffee shop and a children's play area.

## Ulster Folk and Transport Museum

Cultra, Co. Down; ⓣ 028/9042 8428, ⓦ www.magni.org; March–Sept, Mon–Fri 10am–5pm (July–Sept until 6pm), Sat 10am–6pm, Sun 11am–6pm; Oct–Feb closes one hour earlier each day; folk museum or transport museum, adults £4.50, children £2.50, family £12; combined ticket, adult £6, children £3, family £13.

Occupying a huge site straddling the main A2 Belfast–Bangor road, you'll need at least a day to explore these two museums. The Folk Museum is focused on the mythical town of Ballycultra in the early 1900s, whose real buildings have been taken from various parts of Northern Ireland, and is populated by costumed guides. The town also has its own adjacent countryside with farms, cottages and livestock. The Transport Museum has a superb collection of rail and road transport and re-created Belfast street scenes while its "Flight Experience" exhibition examines aviation history through films, aircraft models and engineering interactives. Finally, the Titanic exhibition focuses on the construction in Belfast of the doomed ship, supplying plenty of photographs and contemporary newsreels.

## Down County Museum

English St, Downpatrick, Co. Down; ⓣ 028/4461 5218; ⓦ www.downcountymuseum.com; Mon–Fri 10am–5pm, Sat & Sun 1–5pm; free.

The town's former gaol and Governor's house, built in the eighteenth century, contain some reasonably interesting displays on local history and rather more interesting temporary exhibitions. However, the cell block is certainly worth a visit, each cell having been restored to period conditions and several containing tableaux, such as a group of five men charged with causing an affray at Strangford Pier in 1814 and two women found guilty of passing forged banknotes. Look out for the giant chess and draughts sets in the courtyard!

## Downpatrick Railway Museum

Railway Station, Market St, Downpatrick, Co. Down; ⓣ 028/4461 5779; ⓦ www.downpatricksteamrailway.co.uk; Sat 10am–4pm, also June–Aug Mon–Fri 11am–2pm; prices dependent on type of train trip, child discounts and family tickets available.

The town's old station houses a model railway and displays related to the former Belfast and County Down Railway which ran from Belfast to Newcastle. There are steam train trips on Saturday afternoons in July and August and on some public holidays, plus a special Halloween service and Christmas specials.

## Quoile Countryside Centre

5 Quay Rd, Downpatrick, Co. Down; ☏ 028/4461 3280; April–Aug daily 11am–5pm; Sept–March Sat & Sun 1–5pm; free.

Despite its address, this centre is actually a couple of miles north of Downpatrick, off the A25. Its displays describe the wildlife of the Quoile Pondage which was created when a barrage was built to prevent local flooding, changing the salt-water estuary to a freshwater habitat. Outside there are various woodlands and wetlands to explore and wild fowl to be spotted, along with their nest hidden in reeds on the river-bank. The centre organizes nature rambles and seal-watching sessions on Strangford Lough.

## Murlough National Nature Reserve

Dundrum, Co. Down; ☏ 028/4375 1467, ⓦ www.ntni.org.uk.
Open access all year; May to mid-Sept car £3.10.

Murlough offers a splendid way to enjoy the delights of Dundrum Bay and also provides an alternative (and far more interesting) access to Newcastle beach. There's a self-guided nature trail here which follows a series of paths and board-walks, taking in a variety of butterfly and bird life, as well as plenty of wild flowers and magnificent views of the Mournes.

## Silent Valley

Four miles north of Kilkeel, Co. Down; ☏ 028/9074 1166.
April–Sept 10am–6.30pm; Oct–March 10am–4pm; car £3, adult pedestrian £1.50, child pedestrian £0.50.

The Silent Valley and Ben Crom reservoirs supply much of Belfast and Co. Down's water and a view of the dams themselves makes a terrific sight. The three-mile circular Viewpoint Walk takes in spectacular scenes of the Mourne Mountains while the half-mile Sally Lough stroll takes you up to the dam at Ben Crom (alternatively, there's a shuttle bus May, June & Sept noon–5.45pm, July–Aug noon–6pm; return trip: adults £1.50, children £0.90).

## Ballycopeland Windmill

One mile west of Millisle, Co. Down; ☏ 028/9054 3037, ⓦ www.kingdomsofdown.com/ballycopelandwindmill. July–Aug, Tues & Fri–Sun 2–6pm, Weds & Thurs 10am–1pm; adults £1, children £0.50.

This tower mill dates from the late eighteenth century and was in operation until 1915. Restored and maintained, the mill is the only one still functioning in the county and offers visitors the chance to see how it works and try their hand at milling. The former miller's cottage also has a working model of the mill.

## Coco's Indoor Adventure Playground

27A Central Promenade, Newcastle, Co. Down; ⓣ 028/4372 6226, ⓦ www.cocosplayground.com; June–Aug, daily 10am–9pm; Sept–May Mon–Fri 1.30–8pm, Sat & Sun 10am–8pm; children £3.50, toddlers £2.50.

This indoor soft play area offers a handy alternative on rainy days. There's a variety of slides (including snake, astra and tube), an assault course, a bouncy castle and ball pools while toddlers have their own supervised play area.

## Ark Open Farm

296 Bangor Rd, Newtownards, Co. Down; ⓣ 028/9182 0445, ⓦ www.thearkopenfarm.co.uk; Mon–Sat 10am–6pm, Sun 2–6pm; adults £2.90, children £2.10.

The Ark was Ireland's first public rare breeds farm and features animals such as the Irish Moiled and Kerry cattle, as well as llamas, a variety of ducks and poultry, sheep, goats and pigs (including the Vietnamese pot-bellied breed). There are also both indoor and outdoor children's play areas and a tea-room.

## Exploris Aquarium

The Rope Walk, Castle St, Portaferry, Co. Down; ⓣ 028/4272 8062, ⓦ www.exploris.org.uk. April–Aug Mon–Fri 10am–6pm, Sat 11am–6pm, Sun 1–6pm; Sept–March closes one hour earlier; adults £5.60, children £3.40, family £16.

One of the county's most popular attractions, Exploris provides a real and entertaining insight into the lives of marine creatures. Touch tanks allow visitors to feel and hold creatures as varied as rays and spiny starfish, while an open sea tank (containing a quarter of a million litres of water) reveals a massive range of sea life, including sharks. Elsewhere there's the marine discovery laboratory (where microscopic embryos can be observed) and a jellyfish display. Seals are a regular feature of Strangford Lough and Exploris has recently opened a sanctuary for sick and orphaned seal pups, preparing them for a return to the Lough.

## Tropical Butterfly House and Gardens

Seaforde Demesne, Seaforde, Co. Down; ⓣ 028/4481 1225, ⓦ www.seafordegardens.com; Easter–Sept Mon–Sat 10am–5pm,

Sun 1–6pm; butterfly house: adults £2.80, children £1.70; combined butterfly house and gardens ticket: adults £5, children £2.80.

A trip to the Butterfly House is an absolute must for the chance to see hundreds of giant, brightly coloured free-flying butterflies, as well a variety of somewhat ferocious looking tropical insects and reptiles kept, fortunately, in glass cases. The blissful walled garden includes many rare and beautiful plants, as well as a maze which leads to a pavilion covered in roses

## Castle Ward

Strangford, Co. Down; ℡028/4488 1204, Ⓦwww.ntni.org.uk. Grounds: daily 10am–8pm (Oct–April close at 4pm); adults £3.10, children £1.30, family £7.30. House and wildlife centre: May, Weds–Sun noon–6pm; June–Aug, daily noon–6pm (June, Mon–Fri opens 1pm); Sept–Oct, Sat & Sun noon–6pm; combined house, wildlife centre and grounds ticket – adults £4.70, children £1.80, family £9.90; National Trust.

A little way down the Downpatrick road from Strangford lies Castle Ward, an opulent eighteenth-century mansion set in gorgeous grounds. In June the estate stages and annual opera festival (℡028/9066 1090 for details), but for the rest of the summer season, it's the house which draws fascinated crowds. For children, however, the real attractions are the wildlife centre (which depicts and interprets marine and bird life found around Strangford Lough), the restored corn mill, the many trails and the Victorian playroom. The grounds are a great place for a picnic (there are tables by the lough) and you can camp here too (℡028/4488 1680).

## Armagh Planetarium

College Hill, Armagh city, Co. Armagh; ℡028/3752 4725, Ⓦwww.armaghplanet.com; Mon–Fri 1.45–4.45pm; adults £3, children £2, family £9.

The Planetarium is still undergoing refurbishment and the main reason for visiting is the daily audiovisual show which takes place at 3pm, whose digital projectors take the audience through an absorbing journey through the universe; advance booking recommended.

## Palace Stables Heritage Centre

Friary Rd, Armagh city, Co. Armagh; ℡028/3752 9629, Ⓦwww.visitarmagh.com; Mon–Sat 10am–5pm, Sun 2–5pm (July & Aug opens Sun at 1pm.

Next to the Archbishop's Palace, the former home of the Primates of the Church of Ireland, stands this restored Georgian stable block. Inside there's a permanent theatrical display "A Day in the Life" in which costumed interpreters re-create the day in 1776 when Archbishop Robinson entertained the English agriculturalist and writer Arthur Young, featuring the Archbishop himself, guests and servants. You can also see the servants' tunnel which connected the kitchens to the house (Robinson loathed the smell of cooking) while outside there's a well-preserved icehouse, a sensory garden (featuring wind chimes and fountains) and, by the car park, an adventure playground.

## St Patrick's Trian Visitor Complex

English St, Armagh city, Co. Armagh; ☎028/3752 1801,
Ⓦwww.visitarmagh.com; Mon–Sat 10am–5pm, Sun 2–5pm;
adults £4, children £2.25, family £10.

Apart from containing the tourist office, this complex also houses three multimedia entertainments aimed at children of different ages. In "The Land of Lilliput" a twenty-foot giant tells the story of Gulliver's Travels (whose author, Jonathan Swift, had connections with Armagh). "The Armagh Story" provides a colourful account of the city's history while "Patrick's Testament" is an interactive explanation of the saint's association with the city.

## Lough Neagh Discovery Centre

Oxford Island National Nature Reserve, Craigavon, Co. Armagh;
☎028/3832 2205, Ⓦwww.oxfordisland.com; April–Sept Mon–Sat
10am–6pm, Sun 10am–7pm; Oct–March Weds–Sun 10am–5pm;
adults £4, children £2.

The centre's focus is on the history, culture and ecology of Lough Neagh, but treats its subject in a very lively way, through interactive games and audiovisual shows. There are several miles of trails around the lough as well as birdwatching hides while the centre also provides guided walks and runs an extensive programme of events throughout the year.

## The Argory

Derrycaw Rd, Moy, Co. Armagh; ☎028/8778 4753,
Ⓦwww.ntni.org.uk; grounds: daily 10am–8pm (Oct–April closes
4pm); car £2.10; house: mid-March–May and Sept, Sat & Sun
noon–6pm; June, Mon–Fri 1–6pm, Sat & Sun noon–6pm;
July–Aug, daily noon–6pm; grounds and house tour: adults
£4.10, children £2.10, family £10.40.

Four miles east of Moy, this superb Neoclassical mansion dates from 1824 and sits amidst gorgeous gardens and an expansive wooded estate by the River Blackwater. Still lit by an original 1906 acetylene gas plant, the house's rooms contain an astonishing panoply of original Victorian and Edwardian furniture and period items, including a sumptuous cabinet barrel organ (which actually gets played during special musical house tours – call for details). Various events, such as a Victorian Sunday, are also mounted here each month.

## Ardress House

64 Ardress Rd, Portadown, Co. Armagh; ⓣ028/3885 1236,
ⓦwww.ntni.org.uk; mid-March to May and Sept, Sat & Sun, June
& Aug Weds–Mon 2–6pm; adults £2.80, children £1.40, family £7;
National Trust.

Set deep in apple orchard country, this seventeenth-century
farmhouse, much extended in the following century, can be
enjoyed in the company of costumed guides. The interior
includes a splendid art collection. Children will probably be
more interested in the farmyard and its traditional implements (which can be handled); and there's a playground too,
as well as pleasant gardens and riverside walks. Despite its
postal address the house is actually five miles from Portadown
on the B28 Moy road.

# Sports and activities

## Adventure and activity centres

**Blue Lough Mountain and Watersport Centre**, The Grange
Courtyard, Castlewellan Forest Park, Main St, Castlewellan, Co.
Down, ⓣ028/4377 0715; **Tollymore Mountain Centre**,
Bryansford, Newcastle, Co. Down, ⓣ028/4372 2158, ⓦwww.tol-
lymoremc.com; **Waterside House Activity Centre**, Kinnego Bay,
Craigavon, Co. Armagh, ⓣ028/3832 7573.

## Boat cruises

**Bangor Harbour Boats**, Bangor Marina; ⓣ028/9145 5321,
ⓦwww.kingdomsofdown.com/bangorharbourboats. Offers
pleasure cruises around Belfast Lough and fishing trips from
Easter to October.

**Kinnego Marina**. Boat trips on Lough Neagh. April–Oct, Sat &
Sun, every 30 minutes 1.30–6.30pm; adults £4, children £2.

**Nelson's Boats**, 14B Killaughy Rd, Donaghadee; ⓣ028/9188
3403, ⓦwww.kingdomsofdown.com/nelsonsboats. Runs visits to
the deserted Copeland Islands and offers fishing trips from June
to September.

**Strangford Charter**, 6 Sketrick Island, Killinchy; ⓣ028/9754
1564, ⓦwww.kingdomsofdown.com/strangfordcharter. Operates
a regular tour of Strangford Lough, May–Sept Sat & Sun 3pm; £6
per person.

## Cinemas

**Co Down**: **Bangor Multiplex**, 1 Valentines Rd, Castle Park, Bangor, ☎028/9146 5007; **Iveagh Cinema**, Huntly Rd, Banbridge, ☎028/4066 2423; **Movieland**, Ards Shopping Centre, Blair Main Rd South, Newtownards, ☎028/9182 1000, ⓦwww.movieland.co.uk; **Newry Omniplex Cinema**, Quays Shopping Centre, Albert Basin, Newry, ☎028/3025 2237.
**Co. Armagh: City Film House**, Market Place, Armagh city, Co. Armagh, ☎028/3751 1033; **Centre Point Cinemas**, Portadown Rd, Lurgan, ☎028/3832 4667.

## Go-karting

**Gosford Karting**, 49 Dinnahorra Rd, Markethill, Co. Armagh, ☎028/3755 1248.

## Horseriding

**Co. Down**: **Ardminnan Equestrian Centre**, 15 Ardminnan Rd, Portaferry, ☎028/4277 1321; **Drumgooland House and Equestrian Centre**, 29 Dunnanew Rd, Seaforde, ☎028/4481 1956, ⓦwww.horsetrek-ireland.com; **Gransha Equestrian Centre**, 10 Kerrs Rd, 6 Road Ends, Bangor, ☎028/9181 3313; **Mourne Trail Riding Centre**, 96 Castlewellan Rd, Newcastle, ☎028/4372 4351, ⓦwww.mournetrailridingcentre.com; **Oakwood Riding School**, 24 Benagh Rd, Newry, ☎028/3085 1485; **Tullymurray Equestrian Centre**, 145 Ballydugan Rd, Downpatrick, ☎028/4481 1880.
**Co. Armagh: Greenvale Trekking Centre**, 141 Longfield Rd, Forkhill, ☎028/3088 8314; **Millbrook Equestrian Centre**, 1A Crabtree Hill, Bessbrook, ☎028/3083 8336; **Ring of Gullion Trekking Centre**, Lough Rd, Mullaghbawn, ☎028/3088 9311.

## Swimming

**Newcastle Centre and Tropicana**, 10–14 Central Promenade, Newcastle; ☎028/4372 5034. **Centre**: Mon–Fri 10am–10pm, Sat 10am–5.30pm, Sun 2–6pm; charge for various activities.
**Tropicana**: June–Aug, Sat 11am–5.30pm, Sun 1–6pm; July–Aug, Mon, Weds–Fri 11am–6.45pm, Tues 11am–5pm & 6–8pm; adults £2.50, children under-8 £2, family £12. Warm-water outdoor swimming pool, plus badminton, table tennis, and a crèche for 3–5 year-olds, (July–Aug, Mon–Fri 10.30am–12.30pm & 2–4pm; £3.50 per session) in the adjacent Newcastle Centre. The centre also houses the tourist office and stages a summer concert programme outside, July–Aug Sun 2–4pm; free).

# Accommodation

**Burford Lodge**, 30 Quay St, Ardglass, Co. Down; ℡028/4484 1141, ⓦwww.kingdomsofdown.com/burfordlodge. Very comfortable B&B overlooking the harbour with accommodation at £20 per person and child reductions.

**Burrendale Hotel and Country Club**, 51 Castlewellan Rd, Newcastle, Co. Down; ℡028/4372 2599, ⓦwww.burrendale.com; This very family-friendly hotel has a games room, offers a listening service and organizes various family events throughout the year; from £55 per person plus £10 for each child sharing.

**De-Averell House**, No. 3 Seven Houses, 47 Upper English St, Armagh city, Co. Armagh; ℡028/3751 1213, ⓦwww.deaverell-house.com; Superb en-suite rooms in the centre of the city from £35 per person with a family room at £79 and an innovative basement restaurant.

**Denvir's**, 14–16 English St, Downpatrick, Co. Down; ℡028/4461 2012, ⓦwww.kingdomsofdown.com/denvirs. An old coaching inn with spacious rooms and a very child-friendly restaurant serving sumptuous food; from £27.50 per person, children half-price.

**The Narrows**, 8 Shore Rd, Portaferry; ℡028/4272 8148, ⓦwww.narrows.co.uk; Exceptional guesthouse where every room overlooks Strangford Lough which has a family room at around £90 per night and a splendid restaurant downstairs.

# Places to eat

**The Brass Monkey**, 16 Trevor Hill, Newry, Co. Down; ℡028/3026 3176. Bar redecked in farmhouse fashion with a range of excellent bar, carvery and restaurant meals.

**The Duke**, 7 Duke St, Warrenpoint, Co. Down, ℡028/4175 2084. Astonishingly good bar meals, fresh fish is a speciality) with rather more pricey restaurant options.

**The Famous Grouse**, 16 Ballyhagen Rd, Loughgall, Co. Armagh; ℡028/3889 1778. Justly lauded pub, serving a range of substantial bar and restaurant meals.

**Hearty's Folk Cottage**, Glassdrummond, Co. Armagh; ℡028/3028 1916. Sun 2–6pm; free. There's nowhere quite like Hearty's – a place where you can sit and enjoy traditional music over a pot of tea and a plate of scones and there are plenty of examples of local craftwork on sale too.

**Johnston's Café**, Scotch St, Armagh city, Co. Armagh. Good daytime café with everything from tea and scones to full lunches.

**The Quayside**, The Quay, Ardglass, Co. Down. Fabulous freshly caught fish plus chips, served in this all-day café, plus a grand range of ice creams too.

# 17

# Tyrone and Fermanagh

## Information

Co. Tyrone has tourist offices at: Cookstown, ☎028/8676 6727;
Killymaddy, ☎028/8776 7259; Omagh, ☎028/8224 7831; and
Strabane, ☎028/7188 3735. Websites providing information on
the most visited parts of the county include Ⓦ www
.omagh.gov.uk and Ⓦ www.strabanedc.com.

Co. Fermanagh's only tourist office is in Enniskillen, ☎028/6632
3110, and internet information is online at Ⓦ www.fermanagh-
lakelands.com and Ⓦ www.fermanagh-online.com.

County Tyrone spreads all the way from Lough Neagh
(Ireland's largest lake) in the east to its border with County
Donegal in the west. It's a predominantly rural county whose
main scenic attraction is the Sperrin Mountain range, a wild
and lonely place offering splendid walks, though Omagh is
an attractive small town and makes a fine base for exploring
the region. County Fermanagh's greatest attraction is unquestionably Lough Erne, a complex of waterways and islands
centred upon the cheerful town of Enniskillen. While the
lough offers many opportunities for angling, boating and
watersports, the county also has a number of superb forest
parks, providing enjoyable walks and often splendid views
(contact ☎028/6634 3032 or Ⓦ www.forestserviceni.gov.uk
for details).

### Wellbrook Beetling Mill

20 Wellbrook Rd, Corkhill, Co. Tyrone; ☎028/8674 8210,
Ⓦ www.ntni.org.uk; mid-March to June & Sept Sat & Sun
noon–6pm; July & Aug daily noon–6pm; adults £2.60, children
£1.30, family £5.70; National Trust.

Scutch, hackle and weave in this re-creation of one of the key
components of the Irish linen industry, a working water-driv-
en flax mill whose costumed guides explain how the whole
process worked. As for the beetles, they're not what you might
imagine, but you'll just have to visit to learn the answer!

### An Creagán Visitor Centre

Creggan, Co. Tyrone; ☎028/8076 1112, Ⓦ www.an-creagan.com;
April–Sept daily 11am–6.30pm; Oct–March Mon–Fri
11am–4.30pm; adults £2, children £1, family £5.

Just off the A505 Cookstown–Omagh road, the centre has
been designed to reflect the archaeological sites of the area.
Its interpretative exhibition explores the area's environmental
and archaeological heritage while informing much about its
traditions and culture. The centre also provides details of local
walks and places to hire cycles. It also houses a fine restaurant
and stages a programme of traditional music, dancing and sto-
rytelling events.

## Beaghmore Stone Circles

3 miles north of Dunnamore, Co. Tyrone; open access.

The stone circles are well signposted around four miles east of Creggan on the A505 Omagh–Cookstown road and they're well worthy of a detour to this isolated spot if you are in the area. Tyrone has many archaeological remains, indeed there are more than one thousand standing stones in the Sperrin Mountains alone, but the Beaghmore circles take some beating. None of the stones is more than three feet high; there are seven circles, ten rows and a dozen burial mounds surmounted by cairns. The circles are paired except one, known as Dragon's Teeth, which has over eight hundred stones.

## Aladdin's Kingdom

Mountjoy Rd, Omagh, Co. Tyrone; ⓣ028/8225 1550. Mon–Thurs & Sun 2–7pm, Fri 2–9pm, Sat 10.30am–7pm (opens at 11.30am daily on school holiday weekdays); children Mon–Fri £2, Sat £2.50.

An exciting indoor adventure playground, Aladdin's Kingdom offers a variety of slides, tunnels, rope bridges, climbing frames, a haunted house and a giant ball pool.

## Barrontop Fun Farm

35 Barron Rd, Donemana, Strabane, Co. Tyrone; ⓣ028/7139 8649, ⓦwww/barrontop.com; April–June, Mon–Fri 9.30am–2pm, Sat 9.30am–5pm, Sun 2–5pm; July & Aug Mon–Sat 9.30am–5pm, Sun 2–5pm; Dec Sat 9.30–5pm, Sun 2–5pm; £2.50 per person.

This farm doesn't just offer the chance to see, feed and handle many types of farm animals, but also to say hello to a kangaroo, ostriches, emus and potbellied pigs. There's also an adventure playground and bouncy castle and special pre-Christmas events with Santa and a Nativity show.

## Gortin Glen Forest Park

Gortin, Co, Tyrone; ⓣ028/8167 0666, ⓦwww.forestserviceni.gov.uk; daily 10am–dusk; car £2.50, adult pedestrian £1, child pedestrian £0.50.

Set on the western edge of the Sperrin Mountains, Gortin Glen is one of the North's best forest parks, with a host of possibilities for walkers and mountain bikers or anyone just wanting to enjoy the countryside. There's a five-mile forest drive which offers some breathtaking views of the mountains and three very different waymarked walking trails (none more than a couple of miles in length). There are also three mountain-bike trails and a campsite and a herd of Sika deer.

## Sperrin Heritage Centre

274 Glenelly Rd, Cranagh, Gortin, Co. Tyrone; ⓣ028/8164 8142, ⓦwww.strabanedc.com; April–Oct Mon–Fri 11.30am–5.30pm, Sat 11.30–6pm, Sun 2–6pm; adults £2.30, children £1.40, family £7.10. Cranagh is one of the North's most isolated communities, set deep in the Sperrin Mountains by the Glenelly Valley. The Heritage Centre provides a multimedia account of life in the area, from local customs to the quest for the gold present in the region's rich geological structure. Should you be tempted to join the hunt, the centre will rent you a gold pan (adults £0.65, children £0.35) and direct you towards local streams, but don't give up the day job yet! There's also a very good café here serving excellent home-made food. The centre hosts regular Sunday afternoon traditional music sessions.

## Ulster History Park

Cullion, Gortin, Co. Tyrone; ⓣ028/8164 8188, ⓦwww.omagh.gov.uk/historypark.htm; March, Oct & Nov Mon–Fri 10am–5pm; April–June & Sept daily 10.30am–5.30pm; July & Aug daily 10am–6.30pm; adults £3.75, children £2.50, family £12. Not so much a history of the Irish people as a history of where they lived, the Park features a range of full-scale reconstructions of buildings dating right back to the Stone Age and including a medieval castle and seventeenth-century plantation residence. Inside there are videos and displays which provide further information about the dwellings and their various inhabitants. The Park has a special Family Fun Day in August.

## ExplorErne

Erne Gateway Centre, Belleek, Co. Fermanagh; ⓣ028/6865 8866, ⓦwww.fermanagh-online.com; June–Sept daily 11am–5pm; adults £1, children £0.50, family £2. If you're heading towards Lough Erne and its environs, then this exhibition provides an informative introduction to the area. Various displays and a video tell the story of the lough's formation and its influence on local life and customs. There's also information on local monuments and castles, landscapes and wildlife.

## Brookeborough Vintage Cycle Museum

Main St, Brookeborough, Co. Fermanagh; ⓣ028/8953 1206. Easter–Sept Mon–Fri 5–8pm, Sun 2–8pm; adults £2, children £1, family £5. This ever-expanding collection now holds more than one hundred bicycles and tricycles, including tandems, a butcher's bike and a real old gem from the 1870s powered by levers rather than pedals. There's also a wealth of old toys to see, and the museum's owner has a collection of novelty teapots.

# Enniskillen Castle and Museums

Castle Barracks, Enniskillen, Co. Fermanagh; ⓣ028/6632 5000, ⓦwww.enniskillencastle.co.uk. May–Sept Mon & Sat 2–5pm, Tues–Fri 10am–5pm; July & Aug also Sun 2–5pm; Oct–April Mon 2–5pm, Tues–Fri 10am–5pm; adults £2, children £1.

Enniskillen Castle has played four roles during its six-hundred-year existence. It began its life as a fort of the local Maguire chieftains, then was captured by the English in the early seventeenth century and rebuilt and extended, subsequently becoming a barracks and now containing two museums. The Fermanagh County Museum focuses on local history and wildlife while the Regimental Museum of the Royal Inniskilling Fusiliers celebrates the regiment through a display of its uniforms, flags and military paraphernalia.

# Cole's Monument

Forthill Park, Enniskillen, Co. Fermanagh; ⓣ028/6632 5050; late May to early Sept, daily 1–6pm; adults £0.75, children £0.30.

Built between 1845 and 1857 to honour one of Wellington's generals, Sir Galbraith Lowry-Cole, this monument's 108 steps lead to a viewing platform providing panoramic views of the town and surrounding countryside. Children must be accompanied by adults.

# Marble Arch Caves and Cuilcagh Mountain Park

Florencecourt, Co. Fermanagh; ⓣ028/6634 8855, ⓦwww.fermanagh-online.com; mid-March to June & Sept 10am-4.30pm, July & Aug 10am–5pm; adults £6, children £3, family £14.

A tour of Marble Arch's spectacular cave system lasts for around 75 minutes and commences with a boat journey on a subterranean river. Then you're led through a series of brightly lit chambers whose walls are bedecked with crystallized calcium and crisscrossed by mineral veins, marvelling at an astonishing array of stalactites. Bear in mind that you'll need warm and waterproof clothing and footwear and that tours may be cancelled as a result of heavy rain. Part of the Marble Arch Caves visitor centre is devoted to Cuilcagh Mountain Park (open access) whose shale-covered slopes cross into Co. Leitrim; displays cover the conservation of the park's bogland habitats.

# Devenish Island

Lower Lough Erne, Co. Fermanagh; ferry ⓣ07702 052873; Easter–Sept daily at 10am, 1pm, 3pm & 5pm; adults £2.25, children £1.20.

Devenish is the easiest of Lough Erne's numerous islands to visit and in many ways the most rewarding. The ferry operates from Trory Point, signposted just before the Kesh turn-off on the A32 Enniskillen–Irvinestown road. Once on the island you'll discover the remains of a monastic community, founded in the sixth century, including an oratory, round tower, a thirteenth century church and a ruined priory, as well as one of Ireland's most superb high crosses.

## Castle Archdale Country Park

Lisnarick, Co. Fermanagh; ⊤ 028/6862 1892; park: daily 9am–dusk; free; centre: Easter–June Sat & Sun 11am–6pm; July & Aug Tues–Sun 11am–7pm; free.

Set beside Lower Lough Erne, the park provides a host of activities and possibilities. You can explore the woodland, take lakeside walks or ride around in a rickshaw (£3 per person). Alternatively, bikes can be rented (from £3 for one hour to £10 per day) or you can take on a pony trek (from £4 for a short ride to £12 for an hour; discount for families of five or more). Boats can be rented on the lough (from £25 for two hours to £50 for a day). Alternatively, take the ferry to White Island from the marina (Easter–June, Sat & Sun 11am–1pm; July & Aug, Sat & Sun 11am–6pm: adults £3, children £2) to visit the ruined abbey and its saucy sheila-na-gig statues.

## Crom Estate

Newtownbutler, Co. Fermanagh; ⊤ 028/6773 8118, Ⓦ www.ntni.org.uk. Mid-March to Sept Mon–Sat 10am–6pm (July & Aug extended to 8pm, Sun noon–6pm; grounds and visitor centre, car or boat £4; National Trust.

The vast Crom Estate lies in a magical setting on the eastern shore of Upper Lough Erne. Containing the largest surviving area of oak woodland in Northern Ireland, it focuses firmly upon nature conservation and you can find information and displays on this and the Estate's wildlife in the visitor centre. Fallow deer and the rare pine marten inhabit the woodlands and there are scarce butterflies too. Rowing boats can be rented to explore the lough and its islands and there are seven renovated cottages available for self-catering rental (⊤ 0870/458 4442, Ⓦ www.nationaltrustcottages.co.uk).

## Ulster-American Folk Park

Castletown, Omagh; ⊤ 028/8224 3292, Ⓦ www.folkpark.com; Easter–Sept Mon–Sat 11am–6.30pm, Sun 11.30am–7pm; Oct–Easter Mon–Fri 10.30am–5pm; adults £4, children £2.50, family £10.

One of the most enjoyable attractions in Northern Ireland, this doesn't just recount the history of emigration from Ireland to the USA but re-enacts it. The story of the emigrants is told in the indoor gallery, but it's outside where the real fun lies. Here you'll find original period buildings which

## Lough Erne Cruises

Taking a cruise around Lough Erne is a splendid way to enjoy the waters and staggering vistas of its wooded and hilly shoreline. Several companies offer tours. **Erne Tours**, ⊕028/6632 2882, ⓦwww.discovernorthernireland.com, operates the *MV Kestrel* from the Round "O" Jetty, Brooke Park (just northwest of Enniskillen off the A46). May & June Sun 2.30pm; July & Aug daily 10.30am, 2.15pm & 4.15pm; Sept Tues, Sat & Sun 2.30pm; adults £7, children £4 (£1 reduction per person on 10.30am tour). From mid-May to mid-Sept there's also a Saturday cruise at 6.30pm to The Moorings Restaurant, Bellanaleck (adults £15, children £10 including dinner).

have been moved from other parts of the country or recently constructed replicas and a host of costumed guides populating them and the surrounding "streets". There are thatched buildings, log cabins, a spirit grocery, chapel and meeting house and, best of all, a full-size replica brig, demonstrating the arduous conditions emigrants faced while crossing the Atlantic.

# Sports and activities

### Adventure and activity centres

**Corralea Activity Centre**, Upper Lough MacNean, Belcoo, Co. Fermanagh, ⊕028/6638 6668, ⓦwww.activityireland.com; **Drumrush Watersports Centre**, Boa Island, Kesh, Co. Fermanagh, ⊕028/6863 1578, ⓦwww.drumrush.co.uk; **Lakeland Canoe Centre**, Castle Island, Enniskillen, ⊕028/6632 4250; **Share Holliday Village**, Smith's Strand, Lisnaskea, Co. Fermanagh, ⊕028/6722 2122, ⓦwww.sharevillage.org.

### Bicycle rental

**Co. Tyrone**: Conway Cycles, Loughmacrory, Omagh, ⊕028/8076 1256; An Creagán Visitor Centre, Creggan, ⊕028/8076 1112.
**Co. Fermanagh**: Belleek Bicycle Hire, Belleek Cottages, Main St, Belleek, Co. Fermanagh, ⊕028/6865 8181; Lakeland Canoe Centre, Castle Island, Enniskillen, ⊕028/6632 4250; Manor House Marine, Killadeas, Co. Fermanagh, ⊕028/6862 8100, ⓦwww.manormarine.com;

### Boat Rental

**Belleek Angling Centre**, The Thatch, Main St, Belleek; ⊕028/6865 8181. Rowing boats for £10 per day, £30 with outboard motor.

**Erinona Boats**, Boa Island Bridge, Kesh, Co. Fermanagh; ⓣ028/6863 2328. Rents rowing boats with or without outboard motors for £40 per day, less for shorter periods.

**Manor House Marine**, Killadeas, Co. Fermanagh; ⓣ028/6862 8100, ⓦwww.manormarine.com; Eighteen-foot boats which can take six people (half-day £45, full day £65) and larger "Skipper" boats which can carry eight (£60/£100).

## Cinema

**Enniskillen Omniplex**, Raceview, Factory Rd, Enniskillen, Co. Fermanagh, ⓣ028/6632 4777; **Global**, Oaks Rd, Dungannon, Co. Tyrone, ⓣ028/8772 7733, ⓦwww.globaldungannon.com; **Multiscreen Studios**, Drumquin Rd, Omagh, ⓣ028/8224 2034; **Ritz**, Burn Rd, Cookstown, ⓣ028/8676 5182.

## Go-karting

**Ballynahatty Fastrack Karting**, 3m SW of Omagh, Co. Tyrone; ⓣ028/8225 0170.

## Horseriding

**Co. Tyrone:** Ashlee Riding Centre, 4 Carricklee Rd, Strabane, ⓣ028/7188 2708; Carricklee Equestrian Centre, Urney Rd, Strabane, ⓣ028/7188 3221; Clanabogan Riding School, 85 Clanabogan Rd, Omagh, ⓣ028/8225 2050; Moy Riding School, 131 Derrycaw Rd, Moy, ⓣ028/8778 4440.

**Co. Fermanagh**: Loaneden Equestrian Centre, Highgrove, Muckross Bay, Kesh, ⓣ028/6383 1603; Ulster Lakeland Equestrian Centre, Necarne Castle, Irvinestown, ⓣ028/6862 1919.

## Swimming

**Cookstown Leisure Centre**, Fountain Rd, Cookstown, Co. Tyrone, ⓣ028/8676 3853; **Dungannon Leisure Centre**, Circular Rd, Dungannon, Co. Tyrone, ⓣ028/87753 3252; **Fermanagh Lakeland Forum**, Broadmeadow, Enniskillen, Co. Fermanagh, ⓣ028/6883 1943; **Omagh Leisure Complex**, Old Mountfield Rd, Omagh, Co. Tyrone, ⓣ028/8224 6711.

# Accommodation

**Arch House** Tullyhona, Marble Arch Rd, Florencecourt, Co. Fermanagh; ⓣ028/6634 8452, ⓦwww.archhouse.com; Splendid rural guesthouse offering four spacious en suite family rooms, fine food and a babysitting service; from £19 per person with child reductions.

**Belmore Court,** Tempo Rd, Enniskillen, Co. Fermanagh; ⓣ028/6632 6633, ⓦwww.motel.co.uk. Situated near the town centre, these modern self-catering apartments include two-room family units with a mini-kitchen for £60–65 per night.

**Clanabogan Country House,** 85 Clanabogan Rd, Omagh, Co. Tyrone; ⓣ028/8224 1171, ⓦwww.clanaboganhouse.freeserve.co.uk. Surrounded by spacious woodlands and its own tranquil gardens, this fine B&B offers food and very comfortable accommodation from £25 per person with reductions for children sharing.

**Gortin Accommodation Suite and Activity Centre,** 62 Main St, Gortin, Co. Tyrone; ⓣ028/8164 8346, ⓦwww.gortin.net. Ideally situated near the Sperrin Mountains, this recently constructed centre features a hostel with family rooms from £7.50 per person and self-catering houses from around £200 per week.

**Muckross Lodge,** Muckross Quay, Kesh, Co. Fermanagh; ⓣ028/6863 1887. Set by Lower Lough Erne with a beach at the end of its drive, and its own swimming pool, this friendly B&B offers a babysitting service and has a family room from £17.50 per person with child reductions.

# Places to eat

**The Linen Hall,** Townhall St, Enniskillen, Co. Fermanagh. Part of the Wetherspoon chain, this bar serves very reasonably priced meals and has a special family area at the rear.

**The Mellon Country Inn,** 134 Beltany Rd, Omagh, Co. Tyrone; ⓣ028/8166 1224. Near the Ulster-American Folk Park, this serves a range of bar and restaurant meals, solidly reliant on local produce.

**Oysters Restaurant,** 37 Patrick St, Strabane, Co. Tyrone; ⓣ028/7138 2690. Exceptionally good fish restaurant, serving a range of fishy delights (closed Monday).

**Sarah Jane's Diner,** 41 Main St, Kesh, Co, Fermanagh; ⓣ028/6863 1940. Great café serving good quality fast food and more substantial meals.

# Index

Maps are marked in colour